The Salvation Army
and
the
Children

Authors whose writings are included

General William Booth
General Bramwell Booth
Mrs. Commissioner Frederick (Emma) Booth-Tucker
Commissioner Samuel Logan Brengle
Mrs. Commissioner Theodore (Jane) Kitching
Mrs. Commissioner Sture (Flora) Larsson
Commissioner John D. Waldron
Colonel Catherine Baird
Mrs. Colonel Howard (Sallie) Chesham
Colonel John Larsson
Mrs. Colonel Loyd (Anita) Robb
Lt.-Colonel Cyril Barnes
Lt.-Colonel John Gowans
Lt.-Colonel Ethel B. Rohu
Major Joan Corner
Captain Kitty Wood

Other Works by John D. Waldron:

Women in The Salvation Army
The Privilege of All Believers
The Salvationist and the Atonement
O Boundless Salvation

THE SALVATION ARMY AND THE CHILDREN

*An anthology of selected
articles by various authors
on the place of children
in The Salvation Army's ministry*

*Compiled by
Commissioner John D. Waldron (R)*

The Salvation Army
Literary Department
145 West 15th Street
New York, N.Y. 10011

ISBN 0-89216-060-8

Published by The Salvation Army Literary Department
145 West 15th Street
New York, N.Y. 10011

Printed in the United States of America

Table of Contents

FOREWORD

THIS publication is another anthology of important and meaningful writings by Salvationists and is made possible through the dedicated research efforts of Commissioner John D. Waldron (R).

This anthology, *The Salvation Army and the Children*, reminds the reader of The Salvation Army's historic commitment for the care and development of children through its programs and services.

"Feed my lambs" was a charge given by Jesus. To care for the young and the very young was certainly implied for this was followed by the command "feed my sheep."

The Salvation Army accepts this charge today, as the disciples did 2000 years ago. Here we read of the 1880 beginnings of a positive ministry to children. We follow this progress through the writings of the Army Mother and of those who followed her. We read of successes and problems and failures. Included are ways to guide children as they learn of God's love for them. And we conclude with the poet's plea "let's be better people for little children's sake."

Readers will find in this anthology a wealth of information and inspiration to guide them in their work with children.

Commissioner Orval Taylor
Territorial Commander
Eastern Territory, USA

Introduction

"THE children must be noticed," declared Commissioner Brengle. And noticed they have been, as The Salvation Army around the world has devoted itself to saving the children and shepherding them in a multiplicity of programs. This collection of writings describes both the purpose and the process.

However, this is not a "how to do it" manual for those involved in work with children. The various Youth Departments supply these in abundance, written by experienced, competent Salvationists, in practical, contemporary terms. All those interested in youth work are advised to make full use of the available materials.

This anthology is a collection of Salvationist writings on the importance of work with the boys and girls, written by Army leaders from William Booth to Catherine Baird, from Samuel Logan Brengle to John Larsson. It is designed to provide background information on the beginnings of Salvation Army work among children, by the pioneers who were involved in this historic development, as well as by contemporary leaders.

From these pages you will catch something of the basic philosophy and motivation of all that the Army does for boys and girls. Let us pray that Salvationists everywhere will emulate the example of the Children's Friend, who "set a child in their midst."

JDW

CHAPTER ONE

"The Beginnings of Children's Work"

Ethel B. Rohu

From "John Roberts, Evangelist"

Published by Salvationist Publishing and Supplies, London

1

A N all-alive meeting, and hope to have a good day tomorrow—my first Sunday in Blyth." So ran the entry in John's diary. "O Lord, give me this place!" is the prayer which concludes this entry.

John set about the task as if he intended to help God to answer his prayer. Hearing that a fisherman had been drowned he called at the house to pray with the stricken widow. Five little children with big, wondering eyes were gathered round their mother. Sixty-two years later one of the little girls was to attend a home league rally at an adjacent corps and relate the memory which had lived with her through the years. "He comforted my mother in her sorrow," she said, "and when children's meetings started later on we all joined, and we've been in the Army ever since." She was then sixty-nine.

No place of worship in Blyth was big enough for the crowds who wanted to come to the Army so, whenever possible, the Central Hall, a building accommodating a thousand people, was secured for the Sunday night meeting.

Jack Stoker and his wife were prominent soldiers.

When they were appointed to Bishop Auckland as officers, their farewell meeting was described as "A Hallelujah Concert." They had an outstandingly successful soul-saving career and two of their sons became officers.

The open-air opportunity at Blyth was grand—and seats would be reserved inside for the estimated number who would follow to the indoor meeting. The diary records:

> The people here seem to love having the subject of holiness introduced. They have some knowledge of it, but very little. The clouds are dispersing, however; several have sought and, I believe obtained, this great possession.

Two months slipped by and increasing congregations constituted a problem in accommodation. As the Captain passed the door of the Central Hall on his way to the open-air he saw the people lined up waiting for the doors to be opened. Did his mind revert to his childhood vision of waiting crowds to whom he longed to preach the gospel? The hall would be packed long before the march came in and, alas! many would be turned away. Holding an open-air meeting was possible only because the soldiers' seats were reserved on the platform.

"Announce that no children will be admitted," the local helpers suggested.

"But the mothers cannot come—in many cases—unless they bring their children," the Captain objected.

The hall-keeper registered a resolve to keep out such children as came without their parents as one means of minimizing his dilemma. Then came word from the borough officials regretting that the Central Hall would not be available for The Salvation Army on Sunday evening, July 25th, as there was a prior claim for this date.

4

In this quandary someone suggested asking for the loan of the large Wesleyan Chapel with capacious gallery. The minister was willing, probably trusting that something of the spirit of those Central Hall gatherings would enliven his own charge. Some seats had to be reserved for the usual chapel congregation as well as for the corps soldiery and their open-air adherents. The door-keeper's problem was greater than ever!

The diary entry is somewhat brief. "A grand sight to see that great gallery packed with people, as well as the hall below, but no visible results—though many were evidently under conviction." But there was one result destined to have a more far-reaching effect than could possibly have been foreseen at the time.

As the open-air workers had processioned toward the chapel, a little girl had shyly accosted the Captain and asked, "Please can I get into the meeting tonight?"

"Certainly, if there is room," was the guarded reply.

"Ah, that's just it," she rejoined. "The door-keeper tells me there is no more room." The child awaited eagerly the Captain's decision but, when it came, the light died out of her face.

"If that is the case," he said, "I am afraid you cannot get in." She turned to move away and the Captain, watching the little figure with dejection in every line, thought suddenly of his Lord's words—"Forbid them not...for of such is the Kingdom of Heaven." Long afterward he could recall the thrill that ran through his whole being. He had heard a divine call and, in a flash, a great opportunity was revealed to him.

"Look here!" he said, and the child turned, arrested by his tone. "Would you like to come to a special meeting for children only in the Salvation Army hall, next Friday evening at six o'clock?"

"Oh, yes!" she cried, her face aglow. She was told to tell her schoolfellows and friends and bring as many as she could along with her.

That night in the crowded chapel there was made the first announcement of a Salvation Army meeting for children only.

Among John's papers is a miniature "Manifesto" which he wrote as he sat in his little quarters on the eve of the new undertaking:

> Tomorrow evening, Friday, July 30th, 1880, I am (D.V.) to commence an hour's meeting for children. My object in doing so will be to get them converted. May the Lord help me to accomplish my effort! May He enable me to lead these meetings in a way that shall be interesting and at the same time profitable. I think of beginning with singing and prayer. Then perhaps a little Bible reading showing Jesus blessing the children. I will tell them of His love for the children. Simply—very simply—I will go on to show Him as their Substitute. Explain the long word by illustration of a little boy who became a big boy's substitute in a school.
>
> Ten minutes will be given for Scripture quotation to induce them to learn the Scriptures.
>
> I will tell them of my own conversion in the Sunday-school and so impress upon their minds the fact and need of conversion.
>
> Possibly as we go on I shall get speakers...
>
> Who can tell but what the Lord is now about to save many children, and bring them out into the world as Salvation Army officers? God grant that it may be so, and unto Him alone shall be all the glory. Amen.
>
> (Signed) JOHN ROBERTS.
>
> July 29th, 1880.
> Blyth.

The Captain admitted that it was with fear and trembling that he made his way to the hall—a little before six o'clock on Friday, July 30, 1880. Would there be anyone there? Could that sudden inspiration and announcement have really meant all that it seemed to him to mean?

He was not left long in doubt. As he drew near the hall the sight that met his eyes set his heart beating with pleasurable anticipation. Boys and girls of all sizes and ages were assembling,

6

seemingly in the wake of an invisible Pied Piper. Yes! There was the little inquirer of Sunday night! She was making toward him eager to introduce her own particular friend who was apparently helping to marshal the company. The Captain was pleased to shake hands with the alert little person—perhaps he had visions of her as an officer-to-be. He certainly did not foresee that he was then forging another of those life-links which they who follow the divine call are so wonderfully the unconscious instruments.

This little girl—Minnie Browell, a daughter of the Methodist Manse—brightly explaining that, though she went to the Wesleyan Sunday-school, she had never heard before of a Friday evening school and was so pleased to come, would one day bear a name that became a household word in Poplar. Ten years later, on August 2, 1890, she became the wife of Lax of Poplar, and from thence was at her husband's side in all his ministry.

Of that first children's meeting the Captain wrote: "A glorious time! About seventy present, and I was able to hold their complete attention for half an hour. May the Lord continue to give me the right message for them, so that we may get soldiers and officers for The Salvation Army from among those precious children."

During the days which succeeded the new venture the Captain went about his duties with the ever-recurring thought: "What ought to be the next step?"

Merely to interest the children and make them happy would have no justification unless there were definite results in Army building. "We have been called into being for the salvation of souls," he was always telling the soldiers, "and unless this purpose be achieved our activities are worthless."

Had he given an invitation to the Penitent-form all seventy children would doubtless have come forward—as they would have done anything else that he asked. But this was not the way in which soul-transformations took place. Until he had some evidence of their understanding of what it means to be saved he must close the meeting in prayer and send them home.

But how great a fire a small spark kindles! The children's week-night meetings were becoming the talk of the town. On the following Friday the congregation of boys and girls had risen to 120, and on the third occasion 150 were present. Yet on his return to his quarters, the Captain wrote: "My heart is sad tonight. I covet those children for God's service. Surely some among them will be called to do damage to the devil's kingdom! I am asking the Lord for direct guidance on this imporant matter."

On the following Sunday the direction came. It had been arranged to hold a memorial service for a little girl whose life had borne testimony to the reality of her conversion. The Captain saw the possibilities of the occasion, and spoke of her victorious life and triumphant promotion to Glory as an evidence that children may be saved from sinning and made useful in the service of God.

Among those who came forward were a number of girls and boys. With great joy in his heart and a prayer that he might be led by the Spirit, the Captain dealt personally with all those kneeling in penitence, and the impressiveness of those moments he never forgot.

A second week-night meeting "for children only" was decided upon and each child who came to the Penitent-form received an invitation for Wednesday at six o'clock. This was August 18, 1880.

The Captain saw before him a clear course. Now he would be able to appeal for decisions for Christ to be made in the smaller gathering where it would be possible to have each seeker dealt with individually. In the Friday meeting those who showed evidence of desiring to seek salvation would be encouraged to do so, and also be given an invitation to the Wednesday meeting which was to be the centre of more intensive training in the things of God.

Seldom was there a meeting without someone getting saved. On Wednesday the young converts would testify and, by degrees, they were brought forward to witness in the adult meetings. On Saturday evening they occupied the platform before a packed hall. For those who found it difficult to express their experience the Captain wrote dialogues, being careful that they understood and experienced what they were being given to learn. These extra meetings were included in the reports to the divisional headquarters and arrested the attention of Major Dowdle. Meeting the Captain at an officers' council, he said: "Roberts, have you got children on the brain?"

"No, Major; I have them on my heart," was the reply. Outwardly amused, Dowdle was inwardly touched and interested, as events were to prove.

He arrived on a Friday afternoon, and took tea in the quarters. As six o'clock drew near the Captain said: "Will you be able to find your way to the hall by seven o'clock; I ought to slip off now to meet the children."

"But I want to meet the children also," returned the Major, and together they went off to an occasion both were long to remember.

The Captain recorded: "We had the seats arranged in a square. The children were full of the importance of the occasion. The Major was charmed. He talked like a fiery prophet, and the children leaned forward, wide-eyed and, in some cases, open-mouthed, and listened spellbound. I looked on with a great joy in my heart!"

"Splendid, Roberts!" said the Major. "We will have more of this in the division." The children's case had been won.

From then on the diary records the Captain's movements as

9

opportunity was made for him to travel round the division with a chosen company of saved children to give their witness in public meetings. One of these occasions is noted: "Twenty-nine souls were won for God; week-end collections trebled."

Major Dowdle reported the progress of the work among the children to the General. Hitherto every Salvation Army convert had been commandeered to fight in the open-air battles which preceded each public indoor meeting. These were not military descriptions in name only. The open-air stand was a real battleground; the fort was held in the fire of fierce opposition.

Some would have preferred the quieter service of taking a Sunday-school class but none could be spared, and the running of Sunday-schools was not provided for in the multiplicity of schemes for helping along the salvation war. But the heart and mind of the Founder were ever open to new ventures in soul-saving, and soon after receiving the divisional officer's report he made his way north to look into matters for himself. "These meetings must be started all over the country," was his decision.

Meanwhile, the Captain with the children on his heart was by no means dull to the needs of the adults in his charge. The shipyard had intrigued him from the first survey of its activities. A recent visit to some new docks was noted: "Walked out upon the works where new docks are being built and new roads made. How familiar the scene—tipping wagons, packing sleepers, boys turning points and building themselves huts, boys swearing and quarrelling!" As always after such reflections he wrote his heart's prayer: "O Lord, help me to bring many more—old and young— into the liberty which Thou hast given me."

In all probability the impressions of that afternoon had something to do with "Noonday talks in the shipyard." Of their beginnings the diary records: "Tuesday, October 26th, 1880. Went to the Iron Shipyard to speak to the workmen for the first time. Tremendous disturbance at first, but very soon they got quiet and listened well. Going again tomorrow. O Lord, bring much good out of it!"

The noon meetings at the shipyard became the order of the day. Ministers from the various churches came along to see what was going on, and their services were "roped in." They had awakened to the need and, as Salvationists would say, "caught the fire." We know that one at least, the father of Minnie Browell, became outstanding in his evangelistic ministry.

Overflow meetings on Sunday nights were held in a chapel to accommodate those who could not gain admission to the Central Hall. Then farewell meetings—marching orders had come again!

CHAPTER TWO

"Save the Children"

Emma Booth-Tucker

From "The Cross Our Comfort"

Published by The Salvation Army Book Department, London 1907

I N Christ's tragedy of love, and in that agony of sacrifice, and in that plenitude of grace, certainly the children were not left out!

Nor is there a father or mother among us who would love the cross as we do, if we thought that redemption's great plan had no place in it, no hope in it, no power in it, for the children! But, bless God, in dying for *me*, He died for *mine*!—in dying for *thee*, He died for *thine*!—and in dying for *one*, He died for *all*!

I think I am not far wrong when I say, that apart from the general question of the salvation of mankind, there is not a more important subject before us, as individuals, or as an Organisation, than that of the saving of the young. And I think I am correct when I say that no Society or Church which has as its aim longevity, perpetuity, eternity, can afford to ignore its youth.

One thing is evident—the children exist! If our indifference or neglect of the fact altered it, we should be confronted with a different question. But the fact that the teeming masses of children are to be found in all conditions of society, that they are there for good or for evil, with all the pent-up influences and possibilities for time and eternity within the realm of their capacity, makes the question one of momentous and almost unfathomable importance. If Christianity conquers them they are and must be a bulwark of strength and a tower of progress. If we neglect them they will seize the pillars of our finest spiritual structures and bring them down in shame and discredit.

Speaking of the Church at large, I fear it is not too much to say that while it has been upbuilded, it has likewise been largely destroyed, by its oncoming generations. Oh! when shall we awake to see and to realise what past centuries have failed to apprehend, and failing, have reaped a bitter harvest of spiritual wreckage! Full many a church in the fervour of its first love, despite its paucity of numbers and poverty, has taken hold upon the gates of Heaven, and brought down baptisms of Calvary power, proclaimed with house-top trumpet-note an uttermost salvation, and with sacrificial blaze of holy enthusiasm been ready for anything—everything! But, Eli-like, it has overlooked the importance of bringing within its borders—within the vital touch of a living salvation—the saplings and striplings of its fold, and by and by the young rise up in their worldliness and self-seeking and their money-making, and with their onward tide of energy they sweep down upon the work of the past fifty, eighty, or a hundred years, and bring the temple to the ground, bedraggling the interests and achievements of the Bleeding Lamb in the dust. This *must not be*! Surely, there is desperate zeal and faith enough in our ranks to say "*It shall not be!*"

I heard some figures a little while ago regarding the missionary societies of the world, which at first appalled me, then set me thinking, enlightened me, instructed me, and finally inspired me. I refer to the fact that massing together a large number of missionary societies in heathen lands you will find that ninety per cent of its present-day reinforcements consist of the children of its past converts.

When I was in Paris a few years back they told me that there is not of all that sad multitude—that army of the illegitimate—a foundling which is not claimed by the Church; and thus the child, almost whether it will or will not, swells the ranks of that persuasion.

Then, surely, while there is a needs-be that offences come, and while there will be some who will turn from the fountain-head, and from the lofty standard that God has set before us as a people; surely, surely, I say, we should seize for our Lord and Master at least fifty per cent, or, may I not say, eighty-five per cent, of the children who come under our influence, who touch the fringe of our borders, and who catch the echo of our songs, and claim them for our God and for our Saviour, and for His welfare under our Blood-and-Fire Flag.

It has come to me with much force of late that there is a greater significance, a further-reaching philosophy in those words, "For of such is the Kingdom of Heaven," than we usually recognise. We remember their connexion—how when the disciples would have checked the inrush of the children, the Master sounded the immortal injunction which booms down through the ages and meets us—"Suffer the children to come unto Me, and forbid them not, for of such is the Kingdom of Heaven."

Let us look for a moment at the model which God lifts up—the special characteristics and virtues which the child represents.

And perhaps first upon the list is *simplicity*. In this day, when all the tendency is towards conventionality, and towards a stereotyped appearance rather than a reality, how beautiful, how powerful, how essential as an implement of Gospel service is the simple sincerity of the little child! Among the Romans it was a

17

common practice with the sculptors when they came across a flaw in the marble, or when their chisel accidentally slipped, to fill in the crack with wax. So perfect was the assimilation that only the most experienced eye could detect the fraud. But one simple test existed, the placing of the statue in the sun. Then, alas! for the wax-covered blemishes. The hot rays of an Italian sun quickly exposed the subterfuge. Hence arose the proverbial expression, "sine cera"—*without wax, sincere.* And who among us has not proved that however stammering the utterance, or feeble the capacity, the unwaxed, untutored, childlike outpourings of the new convert's first love wields an influence far beyond that of the most polished or eloquent discourse. Yes, in a thousand different ways, the indefinable touch of simplicity conquers when the combined forces of might utterly fail.

Why should we ignore that peculiar, although perhaps undefinable, force which, entering our ranks, riveting our foundations, and ornamenting our temple structure, shall prove so great an underlying, interlacing force? Simplicity, parent of reality, offspring of sincerity, how great a charm! how unfailing an appeal to the heart of God! how invincible a weapon in the battle for souls! Verily, we see and say with the Master, "Of such is the Kingdom of Heaven."

Nor do the words have less significance when we apply them to the *enterprise* and *energy* of youth.

Who among us has not admired, if not envied, the uncompromising, unhesitating *daring* and *dash* of childhood? Ah! we say, years will follow bringing with them sobering and enlightening effect, and the boy and girl to whom all things seem possible to-day will become the conservative, steady-going pilgrim of to-morrow. But we say it with a tinge of regret in our tone, and with a sigh as over the inevitable in our hearts.

For do we not feel that if the hosts of slumbering sinners are to be awakened from their worldliness and guilt, if the children of light are to keep pace with the powers and plots of darkness, there must be an ever-incoming sweep of that holy, restless, insatiable spirit of fire which burns after all quickest and brightest, and is perhaps manifest most desperately and effectively in the hearts and lives of *the young* of those who, seeing one thing, go for one thing with all that fixedness of purpose, assurance of zeal, and enthusiasm of energy that we find in them of whom it is said, "Of such is the Kingdom of Heaven"?

And, then, look at the *faith* of the little ones! While those older grown argue and criticise, the secret of the Lord is revealed unto babes. While we too often limit the power of the cross and the efficacy of the blood, and the ability of a conquering, keeping Lord, the child cries, "*Speak,* for Thy servant heareth!" and whatsoever He saith unto them, they "do."

Yes, yes! It is this spirit of *simple sincerity;* this spirit of *daring intensity;* this spirit of *overcoming energy;* this spirit of *unquestioning faith;* in all, this spirit of a "little child," that we want in our midst, and without which we shall lose in all those highest, strongest, and most prevailing influences which go to make upon earth the Kingdom of Heaven.

But even if this were not so; even if there were to be no enrichment, no betterment of the Church at large, no increase in numbers to The Army of Blood and Fire by the uprising of a host of sanctified, love-touched, and fire-baptised children in our midst, we should still stand guilty in God's sight if we failed with every power of which we are capable to gather the children in; guilty of neglect; guilty of unbelief; guilty of *disobedience*—for has He not said, "Suffer them to come unto Me," and "*forbid them not*"? Nor did He say it merely to the Christless throng who out of curiosity, or for mere temporary benefit, surrounded Him. No; He was dealing with His disciples (in other words, with His leading officers of that day); with those destined to be the Apostles who should fan the fires of His crucifixion, and enhance the flames of His Calvary passion until its life-giving ray should light the whole world. He said it to those who knew His heart; who had listened to His most powerful teachings; who had witnessed His most telling miracles; who knew something of His soul yearnings for the world; and something of His great plan for its salvation.

And just so He stands among us to-day: we who are forefront in the fray, upon whose spirits the burden of the war presses, and upon whose ears the clash and crash of a thousand claims hourly fall. And amid all our plans and schemes for the ingathering of the parents, He pleads on behalf of the children, "Let them come!— forbid them not!—unto Me!" Not merely within earshot of the tidings of His life and death; not merely within range of a system of theories, or ceremonies, or dogmas; but unto *Him*—a living, personal, saving Christ, who can rectify the young heart as well as the older one, and who can inspire the child Jeremiah as well as the veteran Moses.

Now, The Army takes its stand here, and it will be increasingly powerful and increasingly great in so far as it legislates and labours for the rising generation; in so far as it takes to them and brings to bear upon them the vitalising, renovating, and uplifting forces of a living salvation.

Therefore let those of us who are warriors in the fray gird ourselves afresh for the battle, strong in the conviction that our work will fail to win the Master's approval, and be utterly inadequate to the needs of the hour, unless our efforts result in bringing the children *unto* Him; unless *genuine conversion* is the outcome. Let us remember that the Holy Spirit is pledged to stand behind us, to interpret our words, and to carry home our teachings, and answer our prayers. The Saviour of the lambs knows how to carry them in His bosom; knows how to pierce the little heart with the shaft of His love; knows how to woo even the stripling to the hidden glory and honour of Calvary loss and Calvary triumph.

Children can be saved! Thousands of changed hearts, evidenced by revolutionised lives, are bearing testimony to this fact all over the world to-day, and in many instances, even further miracles of grace are wrought by the child-saint becoming the child-Soldier, and salvation and inspiration for the salvation of others become the growing ambition of the Christ-captured disciple.

It has often been marvellous in my eyes to recognise the early impress of the Spirit's work. Even in babes of two and three years of age I have seen that Jesus has made His presence unmistakably realised.

I remember the case of a baby-girl not two years old who would only go to sleep with her little hand placed through the bars of her cot, "Holding Desus," as she expressed it. And again another who after any little childish wrong or forgetfulnesss would never rest content with the pardon and kiss of those around, but must run to the window, and, gazing up into the skies, with simple baby lispings, would ask forgiveness from the great Parent-heart to whom neither the old nor the young appeal in vain.

Then look at what Church history reveals. Are not the annals that record the deeds and dyings of the martyrs still more eloquent with what the babes and sucklings have suffered? Is not its crimsoned page touched with a pathos which no saint of older growth could have reached? Has not the divine courage of the parent been even outstripped by the immortal heroism of the

21

tender and trembling child, and from that platform of anguish and blood does not the child-martyr proclaim that ours is an all-possible God, and that His salvation is limited not to those who have trodden life's path, and met its dangers and been marred or destroyed by its influences for a certain number of years; but that He who sanctified by His presence the cradle stands by the cradle still, and can inspire those who would come unto Him even from the earliest awakenings of intelligence with the love and grace which shall save unto the uttermost and save unto the end?

Nor are we without witnesses to that power in the present day. No, we thank God for practical proof of the fact that the child of this generation can be awakened to lofty purpose and inspired with self-sacrificing ambition; and while the test of martyrdom is mercifully spared us, we are nevertheless able to rejoice over hundreds of children with whom The Army comes into personal and daily contact whose young hearts are filled with love to God, and whose all-absorbing desire in life is to do what they can for the extension of His Kingdom, while daily striving to gain those further capacities in grace and knowledge which shall make them spiritual giants in the days to come.

God bless the rising Army, and make it a means of bringing in such a floodtide of salvation as the Church of God has never witnessed, and as shall reach the farthest limits of the world's circumference with its cleansing, satisfying, and fertilising force!

CHAPTER THREE

"Confessions of a Grandma"

Flora Larsson

From "From My Treasure Chest"

Published by Salvationist Publishing and Supplies,
London 1981

N O remorse fills my heart as I write these confessions. No contrition wrinkles my brow (though age has done so) and no false modesty can withhold me from the statements I am about to make.

Firstly, very simply, I am grandma to the most wonderful baby in the whole world. And I am *proud* of that fact. But is not pride a besetting sin? If so, I am culpable. I shall have to use picture language to tell you how I felt on reaching this new and dignified status. Had I been a bird I should have winged far up in the highest heaven and poured out my exultant song. Had I been a rosebud I should have opened instantaneously into a perfect flower, filling the room with my fragrance. Had I been a balloon I should have swelled until I burst!

But I was none of these. I was just an ordinary woman to whom this great joy came. What did I do? I did like the woman in Christ's parable of the lost coin. I called on my neighbours to rejoice with me. Only I did it in the modern manner, over the phone. A granddaughter. Alive and kicking. Healthy and whole.

25

Mother and child doing marvellously. What a thrill to give the good news!

Of course, my friends already knew that a great event was in the offing. I could not keep the joyous news to myself. Overflowing with my delicious secret I confided first to one and then another that I should have to be extra careful of my health, for I was an expectant grandmother.

And so the long waiting time began. With both land and sea separating us, my daughter and I wove the old familiar pattern in the form of letters. What to eat or avoid. What to wear. What to prepare. And a hundred other small, intimate details.

What clothes does a new baby need? What are the minimum requirements in the way of equipment? What *does* a new baby wear nowadays? I remember the hand-knitted crossover vests that were the fashion when my first-born arrived. And the long robes he started in. But he was born in England many years ago. My other two children were born in Sweden and had quite a different outfit. They were packed up in parcels, if you understand what I mean. With feet enclosed in the outer covering and a steadying broad linen belt tied round the middle. It certainly made them easier to pick up, as it gave them the firm compactness that a new-born otherwise lacks.

When the first excitement of the news of the new arrival had cooled, another feeling gripped me. A quieter, almost awed mood. Thankfulness to God for a safe deliverance for the young mother and her child. And then wonder—wonder at the miracle of life. I was a link in the chain of the generations of the world. Having received life, I had passed it on, and now my child held her own newborn to her breast. Mystery of mysteries. Out of the great unknown we come, one by one. Back into the beyond we are gathered when our lifespan is at an end.

Of course, I haven't seen the little marvel yet, but I heard her voice over the phone when she was only a week old. Honesty compels me to state that it was a trifle insistent and loud. I hope she will learn to modify it when she grows older. Naturally, I have received photographs of her. It is a cause for real thanksgiving on my part that she does not resemble me in the least. Believe it or not, she is a darling.

Learning early that it is better to give than to receive, she cooed and chuckled in a tape for me at Christmas. No one else around here understands her language of sounds, but I do. She is saying: "Here I am, dear Grandma, safely arrived in this jolly old world. What a lark to be alive, to suck your toes and splash in the bath." And much more. Some of it in a minor key, stridently revealing a funny, empty feeling inside and ... isn't it time we had supper?

My final confession is that I am secretly practising being a grandma. I borrow other people's babies to feel their weight and size up their condition and age. Folk in the supermarket see a grey-haired woman trundling her purchases in a trolley. They have no imagination! I'm wheeling little Anne. Dextrously getting the pram round the corners of heaped-up tins of food and steering in the direction of the fruit. One needs some practice after 20 years without pram-pushing.

One thing makes me a little anxious. The world does not always appear to be the best place for small children to grow up. Scanning the headlines of the morning news makes one apprehensive. So much wrong-doing. So much unmerited suffering. So much heartbreak. And bright-eyed, rosy-cheeked babies have to grow up to face life's burdens. Will mankind never learn the lesson that it must love or perish? My prayers enfold my grandchild daily. May she be one of God's answers to the world's problems.

"Making An Open Road To Officership For Our Own Children"

Jane Kitching

From "The Staff Review"

Published by
The Salvation Army International Headquarters
London July 1925

ALTHOUGH during the years of our married life there have been many occasions, sometimes of weeks and indeed of months, when my husband's duties as an Officer have taken him away from home, and the responsibility for the care and training of our children has fallen the more heavily upon me, I have always realized that his thoughts and his prayers have been with me. This has helped us both to feel that we were hand in hand and heart to heart in the hope that our children would in due course become Officers, should this be—as we believed it would prove—within the will of God.

I can hardly say in respect of some of the matters which have led to the realization of this desire, that we have ever formulated anything of the nature of hard and fast rules. The customs which we have followed—some of them, at any rate—have seemed to come into existence almost of themselves, and have been born, I suppose, of a conviction which has been almost a second nature.

Perhaps, therefore, my best plan will be simply to place upon paper some idea of what those customs have been, leaving my simple account to speak for itself, as to the extent to which we have been governed by any set or pre-conceived plans.

1. *We have made it our pleasure, as much as our duty, to look out for and encourage the first and smallest signs of spiritual concern and of divine life in our children,* and to lead them into a definite experience of Salvation. Coupled with this, we have tried to help them on, as soon as there has been evinced a desire to testify, or to show their colours, or to do anything in the way of work for God and souls—even if for some other young child.

The rate of development often varies greatly in children of the same family, but as signs of progress and growth have come along, and we have heard them utter a few simple words of desire or experience, we have sought to strengthen them in their resolves.

2. *We have not lost sight of the fact that if our children were to accomplish anything for The Army, they must "go through the mill" as Soldiers.* This has meant for us—their parents—that we must ourselves be careful to retain the Soldier-spirit, the fighting spirit which took hold of us in our young days, long before either of us became Officers. To do this, it was evident that we must ourselves take our position as Soldiers in the Corps to which for the time being we were attached, and it was equally evident that we could not hope to do this either happily or successfully unless we saw to it that our love for souls and our pity for the poor and suffering were kept, at any rate, up to the standard of our old Soldier-days.

3. *We have endeavoured to adhere to the principles of The Army in our home life.* Take one aspect of this alone—our pleasures. Our joys in our home life were pure and unadulterated. The briefest excursions to the country or to the seaside brought to the children's minds the possibility of finding real joy quite apart

from, and without having recourse to, the foolish pleasures which the spirit of the world had to offer.

Such matters had to be governed, of course, by the thought of economy. Our income did not permit of undue expenditure, or extravagance in the way of giving the children much in the way of pocket-money—no doubt a good thing for them in the long run! This has found reflection also in the matter of dress. What is the good, especially to the children, of wearing an Army bonnet on Sunday, if one wears a wordly hat on Monday?

I have been pained in visiting some Officers' houses to see but little in the way of pictures and to hear but little in the way of conversation, which would teach or even remind the children about The Army. I was once visiting the home of a Staff Officer of high rank—he and his wife are no longer with us, it is true—in the dining room of which there was not so much as a text of Scripture or a photograph of the General, or any other Army picture to be seen.

4. *We have sought wisdom from God to beware of the snare of education.* We have struggled to give our children the very best we could in this direction, often at no little sacrifice to ourselves, but always keeping in mind the need of showing them that, in acquiring all the knowledge they could, they must do this, not for their worldly prosperity, but in order that it should prove of service to the people amongst whom they might be called upon to labour in the future.

We held this up before them as an ideal—that knowledge was not to be sought for their own ends, but for the purpose of exercising an influence for God and righteousness upon others.

5. *As Salvationists, we have set up a family altar from the day following our marriage.* As the little ones grew old enough, they were taught, one by one, to kneel with us, and in teaching them to pray, we taught them not only to pray for themselves, but for The

33

Army, for its Leaders, for their comrades generally, and for those in trouble and sorrow whom they knew, as well as for the poor, sinning world at large.

It was our invariable custom to have family prayers (or "Reading," as we sometimes called it) immediately after breakfast in the morning, fixing breakfast soon enough to make this possible. An effort to have a similar opportunity with them in the evening had to be adjusted to circumstances, sometimes taking place at tea-time, or later in the evening, according to circumstances of time and season, lessons, and so on, but we always had it at some time.

Usually, it was the Bible or the "Soldiers' Guide" from which we read, though sometimes instead we had an extract from Commissioner Duff's "Life of Jesus," or from a very wonderful little child's Life of Christ which Mrs. Booth gave me, entitled "Jesus, the Carpenter of Nazareth," by a "Friend" named Robert Bird, or from one of a charming series of simple Scriptural stories which includes "Peep of Day," "Line upon Line," "Lines Left Out," "Precept upon Precept," "More about Jesus," followed almost invariably by a "sing," if not a song, and prayer by one of us or one of the children.

6. *We have not thrust anything upon our children that would affect their future, when they have reached an age at which they could, and ought to, decide for themselves.* One by one they have knelt of their own free will at The Army penitent-form. In the battles that have followed, we have, of course, done our best to encourage them. Sometimes it has been in the matter of attending and taking part in the Meetings, outdoors and in; sometimes it has been the question of wearing uniform; sometimes, again, it has been on the point of Local Officership; and as these and other questions have arisen and had to be faced, we have helped them forward. But when it has come to the question of Officership, it

has been, in the case of each one of them, a matter for personal choice and decision.

One of our boys knew of our hope that he would become an Officer, and he desired it himself but he felt that his own wish was not sufficient, unless God called him. He prayed that God would frustrate any step he might take in this direction unless it was the Divine will. There was no hesitation when the call *did* come.

7. *We have magnified the value of Army discipline.* We have always tried to impress upon them that in any position they might hold in the Corps, they must, as Soldiers, or under the terms of their Commissions as Local Officers, be respectful and obedient to their leaders and submit to authority and Regulation, and not give the impression that they desired to be regarded as exceptions because we, their parents, were Officers.

8. *Early in our married life our eyes were opened to the danger created by parents criticizing The Army and its leaders in the presence of their children.* In saying this, I am not thinking of open disloyalty, but of criticism of methods and individuals, in a way that tends to lower the children's estimate of The Army. We wanted our children to feel that The Army was one of God's most wonderful handiworks, that it belonged to Him, and that it held out *an unequalled opportunity* for ministering to the needs of the world.

9. *We have let our children feel that our own estimate of The Army was a high one;* that it stood *unrivalled* amongst other religious organizations. One day, my little girl came home very distressed because a schoolfellow had said to her, "My mother says you children must be awfully common, because you go down to that Army Hall so often, and it is in such a poor street" (years ago it was known as "Knock-'em down" Street). I told my child that she need not trouble about this, and that she could tell her little friend that the reason for our going was our desire to do as

Jesus would have done—to bless and help the children (I was at that time the Young People's Sergeant-Major of the Corps).

In the same way we have made it an occasion to talk at table about The Army and its work, and so to get the children interested in what was already of real interest to us. Surely of all stories Army stories are the fullest of interest, and when my husband has returned from long journeys, one of the first questions which has been put to him has been, "Tell us about the Meetings, and whom you saw, and what you did, Daddy."

Similarly we have shown our interest in what they have told us about *their* work in the Corps, and the cases in which they were particularly interested, and have set to work to help them in their plans for assisting the poor and suffering, feeling that this would feed and strengthen their desire to live for God and The Army.

10. *Then again, in our conversation with and before them, we have not dwelt upon—anyway, I will say we have not empha-sized—the sacrifices and hardships of Army life.* To have done this might only have made them unwilling to accept such experiences for themselves in later years. Our plan has rather been to dwell upon the *joy* and *privilege* of being counted *worthy to carry the Flag,* if not to *bear the cross,* and upon the wonderful joys that ever come to those who choose and stick to the path of separation from the world.

11. *We have prayed that God would save us from discourage-ment in consequence of our young people's mistakes and failures.* These are bound to arise—at least they have in *our* household—scores of times!—but faith and patience, gentleness and firmness, love and prayer have helped us through.

I felt that it was important, in dealing with them about their failures, that they should usually be spoken to alone, and not in the presence of the other children. This is more likely to draw the response which is desired. We must not crush their little hearts

36

when we know that they are reaching out after things that are good and true.

12. *As opportunity has allowed, we have both made ourselves the associates and companions of our children.* Looking back over the years, I believe that this has counted for a great deal. A country walk, a tram or bus ride, a talk about the flowers and the birds, or the shells and the trees, a visit to the Zoo, and a jolly good game, these have all helped to create a bond of union between parents and children, the recollection of which time can never efface.

13. We have had our anxious days as a result of sickness in the home, especially in the case of one of our boys, who for three years was ill at home soon after leaving school. His protracted illness was a great disappointment, both to us and to him, as it seemed unlikely that he would ever be strong enough to accomplish much for God.

We never allowed ourselves, however, to be discouraged, or to discourage him, but tried our best to help him with our faith, and often said, "We believe God will bring you through." There were times when he feared his illness was becoming a burden to us, but we always assured him that this was gladly borne with faith and love and tenderness. He was very fond of these lines:

Art thou weary, tender heart?
  Be glad of pain:
From sorrow sweetest things will grow,
  As flowers from rain.
God knows; and thou shalt have the sun,
When clouds their perfect work have done.

Hope and faith at last triumphed, and the rain has brought the flowers.

I believe that it has been largely due to the adoption of these simple expedients that we have had the joy, I was going to say the holy pride, which has come to us when, one after the other, we have been permitted to visit each one of our children in the Corps at which they have been stationed, and to see how God was helping them—with sincerity of purpose and seeking His guidance and wisdom—to win souls for His Kingdom and lead those whom, in their turn, they were influencing into the path of duty and Soldiership under the Flag.

Our family has been, and is indeed, a great joy!

CHAPTER FIVE

"Saving the Children"

William Booth

From "The Training of Children"

Published by The Salvation Army Printing and
Publishing Offices, London 1884
Reprinted 1976
Schmul Publishers, Salem, Ohio

1. **WHAT important form of training is necessary in order to secure the Salvation of the children?**

They must be led to so yield themselves to God that He shall receive and make them His real children and true servants and soldiers. Nothing must satisfy you short of leading them into the realization and actual enjoyment of all the blessedness concerning which you have already instructed them; in other words, get them CONVERTED, and then give God all the glory for what has been accomplished.

2. How is this to be brought about, or what measures can a parent adopt in order to secure the Salvation of his children?

(1.) *Set yourselves to do it.* Make it the main purpose of your dealings with the children. Keep it in view early and late. *Sacrifice everything that seems to stand in your way.* Count everything gain that will help you, and God will certainly give you the desire of your heart.

(2.) *Take the children by the hand and lead them with you into the presence of God.* Show them how to converse with Him. Tell

41

the Lord aloud, while they kneel by, all about them, and then encourage them to tell the Lord all about themselves. In this way draw out their hearts in actual personal dealing with the Saviour.

(3.) *Do not be influenced for a moment by the notion held by some people that children are not to pray until they are converted.* Men and women, and children too, are to pray anywhere and everywhere, under all circumstances, if they want mercy or anything else at the hands of the Lord. Surely the decree has not gone forth that publicans and little children are not to smite upon their breasts and cry to God to have mercy upon them, because they are sinners. We always thought that was just the reason why they should pray. Therefore, instead of refusing your children the privilege of prayer, urge them to repent and confess their sins to God and ask forgiveness. Make them look into their hearts and lives, and help them to call up to memory their naughty words and ways, and they will go on to remember also naughty feelings and thoughts of which you have no knowledge, and as they look at their sins the Holy Spirit will help them to see how bad they are. Then they will accuse and condemn themselves, and cry for mercy on their own account. Hold them to this. Beware of plastering them with untempered mortar, and crying "Peace! Peace!" when there is no peace.

(4.) *When you feel that they truly repent, show them how to trust the Saviour for a present salvation.* Here you will have little difficulty; children as a rule are simple and sincere, and hopeful. They will readily believe all the truth about their Saviour's love, and easily be led to trust in His glorious person. And when they do so trust Him, He will appear to them as their own Saviour, and they will go into the Kingdom with joy and thanksgiving.

(5.) *Help them to persevere.* The difficulty with children, as with grown-up people, is not to get them started, but to *keep them going forward* in the way of life. Observe here that the perseverance of the children will depend much—

1. On the sort of influences by which they are surrounded, and on the example set before them in their own homes.
2. On their being supplied with wise and judicious teaching.
3. In their having the helps and encouragements which come only from association with adults and children who, like themselves, are saved with a full salvation.

If the children are thus privileged we have no fear for the result. But they must be nursed for God and Heaven spiritually, as you have nursed them bodily, or there is little hope. Let the parents and guardians of children stop and think a little here. Multitudes of children, we have no question, are brought into the Kingdom of Divine grace at a great cost of toil, and tears, and prayer, and then are allowed to float out again, for want of NURSING.

They perish because those who have appointed themselves, or been appointed by the Church, to be nursing fathers and mothers, have not done their duty. We assert, fearless of contradiction, that it is just as important that suitable helps, instructions, and occupations should be provided to keep children marching heavenward, as it is in the first instance to induce them to start in that direction; and it is just as irrational to expect them to be kept going forward in the heavenly way without means being employed to help them, as it would be to expect them in the first instance to be converted without measures adapted to that end.

3. May not children grow up into Salvation without knowing the exact moment of conversion?

Yes, it may be so; and in the future we trust this will be the usual way in which children will be brought into the Kingdom.

When the conditions named in the first pages of this volume

are complied with—when the parents are godly, and the children are surrounded by holy influences and examples from their birth; and trained up in the spirit of their early dedication—they will doubtless come to know and love and trust their Saviour in the ordinary course of things.

The Holy Ghost will take possession of them from the first. Mothers and fathers will, as it were, put them into the Saviour's arms in their swaddling clothes, and He will take them, and bless them, and sanctify them from the very womb, and make them His own, without their knowing the hour or the place when they pass from the kingdom of darkness into the Kingdom of Light. In fact with such little ones it shall never be very dark, for their natural birth shall be, as it were, in the spiritual twilight, which begins with the dim dawn, and increases gradually until the noonday brightness is reached; so answering to the prophetic description, "The path of the just is as the shining light, that shineth more and more unto the perfect day." (Prov. iv. 18.)

4. How can parents best help to keep their children stedfast?

(1.) When the child professes to be converted, and you *have no reason to doubt such profession, at once acknowledge it, and encourage him to confess definitely and boldy what the Lord has done for him.* This will commit him to a life of separation from evil, and help him to persevere. You must remember that a very general unbelief prevails as to the possibility of children having an assurance of any kind as to their being the subjects of the Kingdom of God. If this unbelief *is in your heart* the children will very soon discover it, and you can easily see what a difficult task it will be for them to hold on in the face of the so-called "judgment" (which may be neither more nor less than the unbelief) of those whom they are likely to consider so much better informed than themselves about such matters.

44

(2.) Take the children apart as regularly as you have opportunity, and *pray with them, encouraging them to pray aloud for themselves and everyone about them.*

(3.) *Encourage them to persevere.* Children are very much influenced by their feelings. Nothing, we all know, is more uncertain than feeling, and when, from varied reasons, the children get sad and low-spirited, they will be tempted to think they are not converted after all, and be tempted to cast away their confidence, give way to unbelief, and so lose hope. At such times, and, indeed, at all times, it will be necessary for you to assure them that while they have the inward witness that their hearts are really set on pleasing their Saviour, and while they feel and know that they are obeying Him they should continue to believe that they are accepted and approved by Him. You must insist upon it that they are perfectly right and safe in keeping on believing it, however dark or hard they may feel.

Children need encouraging even more than grown-up people, just because they are ignorant and inexperienced and naturally forgetful, and therefore so easily led off and carried away by the passing amusements and excitements of the hour. But you must not doubt their conversion, or be led away to pronounce it all a mistake, because they display faults, or are occasionally naughty, or disobedient, or irritable, or bad-tempered; that is to say, if they are occasionally overtaken and overcome by their besetting sins.

A beautiful illustration of my meaning came out the other day in the confession of a Little Soldier who had been absent from the meeting, and was visited by her Sergeant. When asked the reason of her absence, she answered in a most dejected tone, "Oh, I've lost it!" meaning her sense of Salvation; "I lost it through slapping the baby." The Sergeant, who was a grown-up Soldier, thought how possible it would be for an adult to lose it if compelled to tug about with a burden, and possibly a fractious one, twice as heavy as her strength was equal to. The Sergeant, however, did not excuse the fault, but rejoiced in the tenderness of conscience which the Holy Spirit had evidently begotten in this poor little girl. She encouraged her to come back to the Saviour confessing her fault, and assured her that Jesus could, and would—if she trusted Him—give her the victory over her temper in future.

Oh, that all parents and guardians and Officers placed in authority over the children would deal with them as wisely—nay, as much in the compassionate spirit of the Lord Jesus Christ—as did this Little Soldiers' Sergeant! If they did, they would have their reward in the perservance of the little Saints whom it is their privilege to watch over. If they do not, let them not be surprised if the goodness of the children is only as the morning cloud and the early dew—no doubt an unquestioned reality while it lasts, but only of short duration, for want of care on the part of those whose business it is to nurse and care for them, and on whose shoulders, therefore, the responsibility of failure rests.

When they are led astray, urge them to come again for forgiveness, *and that at once.* Always remember that children are not capable of disguising their feelings like men and women, but act them out with the greatest simplicity, and consequently you must have all manner of patience with them.

While the main purpose and prevailing spirit of their lives is to please God and do their duty, you are never to be weary in persuading the children to go forward.

(4.) *Encourage the children to tell you the difficulties they have to meet with, and to confess to you when they get wrong, or fall into sin.* Be sure you never refuse to hear or advise with them on such matters. On the contrary, bear with them most patiently. Advise them how to resist their temptations and surmount their difficulties, and encourage them again and again with the most

46

positive assurances of success if they will persevere. Cultivate the greatest freedom in speaking with them on spiritual matters, until the natural diffidence of their hearts to talk about spiritual things is broken down and destroyed for ever. By pursuing this course it will soon become just as natural for them to talk to you about their spiritual, as it is about their temporal interests. It is usually pride, or shame, or satanic influence, or unbelief which prevents people from conversing on spiritual things, and you should take every means to destroy these fatal influences out of the hearts of your children. NOTHING IS MORE IMPORTANT to the spiritual welfare of children than keeping the freest possible intercourse open between them and their godly parents.

As we have travelled about the country we have observed in many families the greatest diffidence and awkwardness in conversing about spiritual matters. People will talk to each other about their church or chapel, or *about* religion in a general sort of way, but the interests of *their own souls* are never alluded to in a straightforward manner. Indeed, so far as any personal dealing or direct conversation goes, about individual Salvation, the daily intercourse of many families would be just about the same had they not got any souls at all—as if they had not to go up together to the judgment seat of Christ, and afterwards live for ever in Heaven or Hell.

We have known fathers and mothers—professors of religion of years' standing, sometimes high officials in churches—who could not by any means screw up their courage to speak directly to *their own* children, or even to each other, on the subject of personal Salvation. We have seen these people, when the great questions of Salvation and damnation have been pressed home upon their attention by the powerful influences of great religious awakenings, compelled to *write letters* to their sons and daughters, setting forth the importance of their coming out for God and

47

getting right with Him!! They feel they must do something—very proper they should—and we suppose they had better do it in this way then not at all.

But what an unnatural, stiff, stand-off, unscriptural, un-Christlike sort of religious atmosphere is this for parents and children to have grown up together in! Can this be supposed for a moment to be the right kind of *family religion?* "Is this the NURTURE and ADMONITION of the Lord"? Never! It looks much more like the nurture of the ostrich or the cuckoo, which are said to leave the nursing of their young to the tender mercy of chance, and far more akin to professional indifference than to the warm, happy freedom wherewith Christ makes His people free.

The mother can talk to her child, and the father to his son, on all the range of worldly topics with the greatest ease and pleasure, and that from their earliest days. And the topic of Salvation should certainly be more frequently and fully dealt with than any other. When it is thus, no such wall of separation as we have been describing can possibly grow up between parents and children, or between brothers and sisters, on divine and eternal themes.

(5.) *Read the Bible with your children regularly.* So soon as they can comprehend, explain to them that God has Himself caused this Book to be written, to teach and guide them. Create for it in their hearts the greatest respect and reverence.

Read a short portion at a time. When they can read themselves it is wise to let them read aloud with you, verse by verse. In doing so, strive to keep their attention. Always remember how easily their minds are taken off by passing thoughts, so that you should be continually watching to find out whether they are attending to what is being read.

Carefully explain the meaning of what you read: better read one verse, or half a one, and make the children *understand* it, than twenty without. Never take for granted that children understand a thing because it has been explained to them before, or because they don't tell you at the time they do not understand it, or because they ought to understand it, or because you understood it at their age. Always bear in mind how forgetful children are, and how busy the devil is to steal away the good seed that has been already sown: and go on patiently repeating and repeating yourself until they do remember and do understand.

Always make what you read *interesting,* because if you do not you might as well save your labour and keep the Bible away from the children. No greater injury can be done to them than to so read and teach the Bible as to surfeit them with it, and make it a distasteful book. It is a question whether it would not be better *not* to teach it at all, and let them grow up totally ignorant of its sublime facts and principles than to so *bore* them with it that they shall be made to hate and avoid it afterwards, which we are afraid is the case with very much Bible teaching.

Always apply what you read to their own personal experience and condition so far as their experience and condition are known to you, and to the facts of everyday life around them. We fancy the Bible is very often so presented to children as to make them grow up with the notion that it was once a very important book, having in it a number of statements, sentiments, and doctrines, that were very applicable to a people who lived a long time ago; but that it has very little relation *to them* so far as *their* everyday joys and sorrows are concerned: in short, that it is an old fashioned book, altogether out of date now-a-days. Now you should explain and apply the Bible, showing how the people of ancient times were men and women such as you are; that the child-life then was just the same sort of life, having just the same trials and difficulties, as child-life has to-day. Show them that God is no respecter of persons, and that the same conduct now, as then, will bring with it the same blessing or the same curse. To so read the Bible to your

49

children as to make them feel that it is *their* book, intended by God to be the guide of *their* youth, is a very important and necessary duty.

This course should be taken with all your children, whether you have reason to hope that they are converted or not.

(6.) *See that the children regularly attend religious meetings adapted to their age and intelligence, where such are within their reach.*

As a rule, the regular services of ordinary Churches and Chapels are above their comprehension, and inspire them with very little interest. They are consequently altogether outside their sympathies, and the children neither understand nor care for them; their minds, not being able to take in the meaning of the discourse, or to feel any interest in the ceremonial, wander off to their toys, and games, and lessons, and all the other little interests of their daily life. It is perfectly natural that it should be so. The services are not in any shape or form intended for children. They are meant to meet the need of people of thought, intelligence, and experience in all the difficulties of religious life and all the controversies of the day, about which the little ones know nothing, and, if it were possible, care still less.

If we were asked to advise parents how they should act in such a case, we should feel somewhat at a loss to answer. In our own family, before we knew The Salvation Army, we may say we always supplemented the regular adult service with a meeting held with the children themselves, in which hymns, and prayers, and scriptural explanations were given adapted to their age, experience, and intelligence. This meeting was usually conducted by their mother, the children being encouraged to take an active part themselves.

Salvationists, for whom these directions are more specially written, have great advantages in this respect as to public meetings. The Army services are usually within the capacity and interest of children, because the prayers, songs, addresses, and scriptural explanations are so uniformly spoken to the heart, and measured and adapted to the intelligence of ordinary working people. All the exercises are made short, lively, and simple, and beyond all this, they are usually attended with those influences of the Holy Spirit to which children's hearts are specially susceptible. Little Soldiers' meetings, where properly and effectively conducted, are better still.

5. Is there not sometimes a difficulty in forming a correct judgment as to whether children are really converted, even when they profess to be?

Yes, undoubtedly there is; but unless the conduct of the children unmistakeably contradicts such a profession, we should always interpret it in the most hopeful manner. Great care is required in *this direction,* as we have already intimated. It is perfectly natural to suppose that Satan should attack children after the same fashion as he does grown-up people, and one of his common devices is to seek to create doubts as to the *reality* of the change which has been experienced.

You must beware of allowing the devil in any shape or form to make you his ally in leading your children into doubt and fear on the question. Beware also of making your experience, or the experience of older people, the standard for the children. If there is any ground to hope that God has operated, and is still operating on their hearts, by all means give them the benefit of that hope, and rely upon the teaching and Power of the Holy Spirit to rectify what seems to you to be wrong and wanting in them, and to lead them into all needed truth and Salvation.

6. What should be done with children who, after making a profession of Salvation, backslide and fall into sin?

What do you do with children who, after being washed and dressed and sent out for a walk, slip and fall on the dirty, muddy road? You answer, "We help them up again, wash them, and put a plaster on the sore place if one has been made by the fall." Well, we say, act just after the same fashion when your children have the misfortune to stumble and dirty themselves spiritually by falling into sin, and so come again under the power of the devil. Run after them; pity and pray for them; help them up again; lead them to the cleansing Blood, and encourage them to hope that the same calamity shall never happen again. *Do this just as often in one case as you would in the other,* and if you persevere the child will get right again, and in a little time grow stronger and learn to go out even on to slippery places and not fall; nay, in a little season he shall run and not be weary, walk, and not faint.

But when your children slip and come to grief, little or nothing is gained by upbraiding or scolding them, and still less by telling them that *you expected it would be so.* We cannot conceive of any method much more likely to serve the interests of the devil and drive your children to despair, than letting them see that you have no faith in their being able to persevere.

Surely the beautiful parable of the Saviour with regard to the wandering sheep is applicable to parents and worthy of their imitation with respect to their own children, if it is applicable to any Christian shepherds at all. If father or mother has a lamb that leaves the fold and wanders, in heart, away on to the mountains, they ought to act on the counsels laid down, follow it into the wilderness, and with pity, and tenderness, and rejoicing bring it in their arms into the fold again.

7. Is it surprising that of the small number of children who make any profession of religion, so few endure to the end?

Not in the least, seeing that the children have very great difficulties in their way.

(1.) Children, in common with adults, *have to fight against the world, the flesh, and the devil.*

(2.) Children *have to contend with the depressing influences arising from the common unbelief* of adult Christians as to whether young people *can* be converted, or whether they are converted when they profess to be.

(3.) *There are literally no arrangements in ordinary churches or family organisations to help the children* in the hard fight they have to make against their enemies.

(4.) *Children are so inexperienced* as to the nature of evil that they are continually being taken by surprise, falling into traps and snares concerning which they have never had the opportunity of hearing anything.

(5.) Children, being so *naturally light-hearted, are easily led away into folly and frivolity,* by which they grieve the Holy Spirit and bring themselves into condemnation.

(6.) Children are *so affectionate and so anxious to please* those whom they love, that they are often induced to do things that are doubtful from sheer kindness of heart.

(7.) Children, *as a rule, are so sincere that it is not only distasteful, but almost impossible, for them to play a part.* The moment they come to feel they have done wrong they throw up the profession of religion, go away into unbelief and despair, and accept the notion everywhere prevalent that real godliness is impossible to little children.

If you want to keep your children, watch them and condescend to be at some trouble to understand them and the difficulties that strew the pathway their little feet have to tread in order to reach the heavenly shore. Many parents carry their heads so high that they forget the slippery paths of their own youth, neither considering the danger of their own darlings nor helping them to escape it.

Be assured, however, that not only can your children be saved, but they can be kept—if you will be at the trouble.

8. But do not these counsels go on the assumption that the Salvation of the children is very much a human affair?

We do not wish it to be thought so. On the contrary, we wish it to be understood all the way through that the Salvation of children, as of grown-up people, is only accomplished by the Power of the Holy Ghost through the precious Blood of the Lord Jesus Christ.

If the children are ever saved, or kept saved, whether for a day only, or for ever, it will only be by the Power of God. At the same time we do wish it to be understood that Salvation is conditional. If the children repent and believe, they will be converted; that is, if they are old enough to understand what repentance and faith are, or to practise them, understood or not. And if their parents use suitable means, and pray and believe and watch over them, they will not only be saved, but kept by the Power of God unto everlasting life.

It is in the kingdom of grace as in the kingdom of nature—the kingdoms are but one—if you plough and sow and harrow you shall reap, but your seed will quicken and grow and ripen all the same by the Power of God.

CHAPTER SIX

"The Core Of Our Message"

Catherine Baird

From "Of Such Is The Kingdom"

*Published by Salvationist Publishing and Supplies,
London 1948*

ONE day when Jesus had been preaching in the synagogue, a Hebrew lawyer, whose chief duty in Israel was to expound and interpret the Jewish law, asked Him: "What must I do to inherit eternal life?" Jesus questioned the man concerning the scriptures, whereupon the lawyer repeated those two commandments which our Lord said were the greatest of all:

> Thou shalt love the Lord thy God with all thy heart, and with all thy soul, and with all thy strength, and with all thy mind; and thy neighbour as thyself. "This do," added the Master, "and thou shalt live." (Luke x.27,28.)

All that The Salvation Army teaches those children who come within its influence is based upon the belief that a full and abundant life depends upon a human being living in accordance with the principles set forth in these commands: love for God resulting in love and service for others.

In a simple message to children published in *The Young Soldier* in 1897, William Booth, the Army's Founder, wrote:

> I want you to be friends of God.
> I want you to have good hearts.
> I want you to live useful lives.

To the Army's Founder a "useful life" was a life spent for mankind.

In harmony with their desires for their children, parents, so far as lies in their power, usually make plans for their education. And, to any careful student of what the Army of to-day is teaching its children, it is evident that this has evolved out of what the Founder and the Army Mother, as a result of their own high desires for children, set before them.

The Army has a definite plan, prepared in detail, with the idea of leading the children into a right conception of God and His will for mankind. Only this, we believe, will create in the hearts of boys and girls a longing for friendship with God. To bring about the desired result the teacher is urged to seek to show God *as He is,* and not as the teacher in his own childhood may have thought Him to be. In the *Primary Manual* we read:

> Finally, when teaching the Old Testament, avoid dwelling on unpleasant or frightening details in the scripture story, e.g., the cutting off of Goliath's head by David, or the massacre of the priests of Baal by Elijah. Primary children cannot be expected to understand the distinction we make between man's imperfect understanding of God in the Old Testament, and the complete and final revelation of Him given by Jesus in the New Testament.

The Army, it will therefore be seen, teaches that a true conception of God can be reached only through a knowledge of Jesus Christ, in whose personality the face of God is seen, and in whose way of life God's will for the human race is shown.

The Army teaches that a child may know God, may see Him in Jesus, and, through a vision of His goodness and beauty, become aware of wrong-doing and have a capacity for repentance, seeking forgiveness and turning from evil to good, becoming a follower of Christ—which means striving to put into practice those truths which the Master taught.

The Army teaches that there can be no substitute for a personal relationship with God. From the "Directory" class, where children are introduced to Bible doctrine and Salvation Army principles, to the company meeting where they are instructed in the scriptures, the dominant theme is personal experience of God. Though the method of teaching and the nature of the Army's many branches of work among the young vary to meet the need of age and temperament, all are a means to the same end.

Concern lest anything should interfere with the child's relationship with God influenced William Booth in such momentous decisions as that made by him after having sought to know God's will for the Army in the matter of whether or not Salvationists should observe the sacraments.

The Army's Founder had been baptized in the Anglican communion. He had known the joy of worshipping through the sacraments. Yet, as leader of an Army of men and women, redeemed in some cases from the grossest sins, he felt that only confusion and loss might result from observing what seemed to him to be merely symbols of a real experience. Baptism by water, for instance, was only the shadow of immersion by God's Holy Spirit.

So for infant baptism the Founder substituted the beautiful dedication ceremony known to every Salvationist. The child is not sprinkled with water but, like the young Samuel, brought to the "tabernacle" and "given to God." This act is not his but the parents'. Like Samuel the child is, as it were, brought up in the house of the Lord and accustomed to its sacred vessels.

The story of Samuel related in the Scriptures might well be the story of many children who attend the company meeting—children of all races and classes. Dedicated to God by Hannah, he ministered to Eli in God's house. Yet it is written: "Now Samuel did not know the Lord, neither was the word of the Lord yet revealed unto him." (I Samuel iii. 7.)

So, when the Voice called, the lad took it for a human voice

59

and ran to Eli from whence he had hitherto received his orders. And it was a human voice that helped him to see that God was speaking directly to him, and that he was about to enter into the personal experience of God which his mother had desired for him.

That the Army has not been mistaken in its belief that children may know God and be converted has been proved by scores of instances of children making a definite choice and spending all their years in serving God.

The Founder wrote: "Take the children by the hand and lead them into the presence of God. Show them how to converse with Him." And again: "Nothing must satisfy you short of leading them into the realization and actual enjoyment of all the blessedness in which you have already instructed them; in other words, get them converted."

The Army teaches that friendship with God is the happiest experience that can come to a child or to man. The Army Mother, addressing those who had the responsibility for teaching and training children, was anxious that they should *enjoy* religion. In those early days, when the learning of Bible chapters was often demanded as a punishment for some mischief, what she said must have seemed quite revolutionary!

> If you want your child to love and enjoy the Sabbath you must make it the most interesting day of the week. If you want him to love and read his Bible you must tell its stories and elucidate its lessons as to make it interest him. If you want him to love prayer you must so pray as to interest him, and draw out his mind and heart with your own, and teach him to come to God as he comes to you, in his own natural voice and manner, and tell Him his wants and express to Him his joys and sorrows. The themes of religion are of all themes the most interesting to children when dealt with naturally and interestingly.

The Army teaches its children that the Christian life is one of growth, and that one does not, after having started out on the good life, suddenly become perfect. It is a life of development, during which, as a person's conception of God becomes clearer, he

60

progresses. Perfection, in the spiritual sense, means healthiness at each stage of development.

This idea was doubtless in the mind of the Founder when he said: "I want you to have good hearts." He meant healthy hearts; hearts that are true, complete, honest. To this end the Army teaches that religion is without meaning if it does not come from within and therefore show in every detail of life, and that the converted child shall seek to put Christian principles into his play, his lessons, his work and his relationships with other children. Goodness or healthiness of heart expresses itself in good work rather than in words, or in forms and ceremonies. Love for God is shown by love toward others more than in songs of praise. The good life must be lived, or it cannot be preached. "Man looketh on the outward appearance, but the Lord looketh on the heart," is a statement emphasized in Salvation Army teaching for children.

Addressing a crowd of teen-age young people in London in the year 1898, Bramwell Booth, then Chief of the Staff, said:

> I expect some of you will be very much better officers than the officers we have now; but you will have to wake up. To do the things that are small and insignificant and to do them as well as the great things and with the same zeal, is important. Nothing is little in the sight of God. If you are set to wash up a tea-cup, or put a penny stamp on a letter, or dust a table, or put on a pair of clean boots, or write a letter, it is all the same in the sight of God. The boy whose duty it is to clean my boots, who cleans them properly and puts some steam into it, can make that just as acceptable, just as pleasant and agreeable to God and just as profitable to himself as if he were to preach a sermon in the Exeter Hall. It is just as important to the boy who has to clean my shoes, just as important for his salvation and for the salvation of the world that he cleans them as well as they can be cleaned, as it is important for the world's salvation and the General's that, when he stands up in Exeter Hall before 3,000 people, he should preach as well as he can.

> Later, he said:
> If you are to sweep a floor, sweep it so that if the Archangel came with his heavenly broom there should be nothing left for him to sweep up. If you are a cook, cook the pudding so that everybody who has a bit will say, "We must

have another pudding like that!" If you are an errand boy, go your errands, finish them off, come back. Do them so that the people who employ you can say, "We have got an errand boy here who can lick creation!"

If any one thinks such teaching unnecessary, he has but to look around him for examples of young people whose main idea is to escape responsibility. A stenographer came back to the city from a holiday weekend weary from late parties. She asked a friend to telephone her employer and say she was ill. The friend did so and the two girls laughed over the sympathy of the unsuspecting "boss." Neither thought she had done anything amiss.

A successful professional man, with a son at a well-known public school, told with relish how he had "fooled the head-master" with a false reason for bringing his son home to his sister's birthday dance. The father, and of course the boy who idolizes him, thought he had done something clever.

A group of boys laughed uproariously when they heard someone berating the promoter of gambling who makes himself rich through other people's losses. "Good for him!" they cried, cheering and clapping. "He's a smart guy!"

The boy or girl who learns that the natural consequence of goodness is good work serves his neighbour; he has neither desire nor intention to cheat him.

The Army teaches that the good life means giving up to God body, mind and spirit. As the soul is guarded, so also must the body be cared for as the fine instrument that serves mind and spirit. The Army urges temperance, self-control and abstinence from any habits likely to injure the body, weaken the will, or lessen the child's sense of self-respect. Body, soul and spirit are a trinity, each affecting the other. Each is hindered and made less useful if the other is abused or neglected.

The Founder's third desire—that children should live useful lives—meant, first of all, that they should serve God and that they might early set so high a value upon doing the will of God that no promise of position, favour, or material reward could cause them to depart from it, or to waver either in their choice between right and wrong or between good and best. The Army's children are taught that neither position nor authority nor wealth will make them powerful, but goodness and usefulness. To Salvationists, power means effectiveness and, for an individual to be effective, he must fulfill the purpose for which he was made—that of glorifying or showing forth God and by so doing winning others for His cause.

To serve God is to serve man, particularly the lowest and the neediest. No child is too young to take part in this experience. Out of the belief that the young are happiest when at work on something constructive came the many activities for them which are now a part of our organization.

The Army believes that its duty toward children is to teach the impressionable the truth about God, and that every young people's worker should use all his ingenuity to do so. The teacher's work is to arm them at the commencement with what knowledge a mind in the making can absorb about God, who Himself will fit the young to take part in life.

The Army seeks, not to impress children that God is watching to "catch them out" and to punish them for wrong, but that, because He loves them, His eye is ever upon them. Further, that He uses His power not to destroy, but to create and to commune with man, the greatest and noblest of all His creations. Again, that truthfulness is desirable, not merely because liars will be punished, but because lying is like chipping pieces off a finished work of art or daubing inharmonious splashes on a masterpiece.

The Army teaches that friendship with God is not a way of escape from the world, but a means of gathering inward strength which will make those who possess it triumph over sin.

The Army believes that as, when you teach a child to read, you do not give him the classics, but begin with the A B C, so you should do with religion. The A B C of religious experience is knowing that God is love. It is not easy to teach small people that which is abstract, but they can readily understand the deeds that love does. And where can we find perfect love operating through body and soul except in Jesus Christ? He showed men how to bring Heaven into every common task and to establish the Kingdom of God now, for with His whole self He loved the Father, and for His neighbour He suffered death on the cross.

We cannot expect children to understand the great mystery of the Atonement; but, believing with our whole being that in Him alone is their salvation, we bring these little ones to Jesus.

CHAPTER SEVEN

Excerpts from:

"The Children and the Young People's Work"

Bramwell Booth

From "The Staff Review"

Published by The Salvation Army, International Headquarters, London July, 1924

THE work of The Army for the Salvation of children really began in the home of the Founders. There is no doubt that the Army Mother even before her marriage entertained very definite views about the work of Divine Grace in the hearts of little children. Her own conversion when a girl at school, and the desire which forthwith took possession of her to make her Saviour known, left her also with little question about the service which could be rendered by the young to the cause of Christ. But it was in her own home and amongst her own children that she was to see the practical working out of many of the things which she had believed and hoped from her earliest days. I feel no doubt whatever that in any circumstances she would have deeply impressed on her children the claims of God as she saw them, and I believe she spoke the literal truth when she said: "I will not have a wicked child!" She used to pray in the very presence of her children that she might rather have to lay them in an early grave than to mourn over one who had deserted the path of righteousness.

That their children were won for Christ and that the change which was seen in those children's lives after their Salvation greatly confirmed and encouraged both parents in their faith for children generally, we know to have been the case from Catherine Booth's own testimony. "If *our* children may be thus transformed," she argued, "why not many others, and if many others why not all! Let us call the children to their Saviour's side and plant their feet upon the Rock."

Her own children had given her great joy. She regarded them as good children measured even by her high standards, and the very fact that she could and did apply her own vigorous—at times even severe—(I speak from experience!) methods of training is in itself a tribute to their early development in much that belongs to what we all value. But she did not for one moment allow this to obscure the fact—the dominating fact—that they must repent and be converted, that they must be born again of the Spirit if they were to be saved. The thought was ever present to her mind, the prayer for their *Salvation* was ever on her lips. *They* also knew—they felt from the very dawn of intelligence that she believed they could be saved—that she was praying and labouring to bring them to Christ.

The Army Mother saw her children go one by one, as the Founder says, into the Kingdom with joy and thanksgiving.

But I am thinking of something more than this when I say that the work of The Army for the young began in the Founder's home. While their four elder children were still between ten and fifteen years of age they began to invite their acquaintances and the children of neighbours to visit their schoolroom at Gore Road and to hear from them the strange sweet story of a Saviour's love shed abroad in the heart of a child. Those occasional and very small and at first quite "unorganized" gatherings were different in almost every particular from the "children's services" which the Founder had often included in his special missions in the various towns. The only thing they had in common was an earnest desire and appeal that someone should decide for Christ. Nevertheless those meetings had an important result. They convinced the Army Mother, and her influence prevailed with the Founder himself, that it would be possible to organize and sustain a regular work for the Salvation of children *by means of the children themselves.* From that moment, 1871, efforts began with this end in view. Tentative plans were made, experiments were tried, special campaigns—all, or nearly all, in a small way—were instituted, always with these objects: (1) the immediate Salvation of the children by faith in Jesus, and (2) their organization and training to do work for the Salvation of other children.

Soon after this a Lay Secretary of the Mission named Rapson began to interest himself in this work and was appointed to organize it. A small Hall in the East of London (Thomas's Passage) was placed at his disposal, and Meetings were held regularly on Sundays and on two or three nights of the week. The neighbourhood was a very rough one. The police were obtrusively unfriendly and the juvenile portion of the population practically heathen as regards respect for any form of religion. The meetings, always (if we so permitted) crowded on Sundays, were more or less disorderly, sometimes even riotous. But they were nevertheless wonderfully blessed. Children—ordinary boys and girls— were saved, and at once took their stand for Christ. Some of them, with whom I became personally acquainted, suffered cruel ill treatment at the hands of their former companions as well as from their parents, and yet stood firm in their new joy and love. Presently not a few of their persecutors were led to Christ through their influence. Small meetings were held on the week evenings for instruction and for prayer and testimony, some especially in preparation, week by week, for the coming Sunday. Always the greatest impression was produced on even the most disorderly gatherings by the saved children's own testimonies which often ran something as follows, though I cannot of course pretend to reproduce correctly the East End terminology or pronunciation of those days. A boy of twelve or thirteen, known perhaps as "Happy Arthur" or "Praying Tim," would say:

> *I say, you boys, just listen half a minute . . . . You know I was always getting into scrapes, you know I often did you in at "two and one" (a kind of pavement game at that time with marbles). (A howl of derision here.) Well, I say, look 'ere—you know I don't do it now—do I? (dead silence). Even Mother says I am different and she has stopped "sugaring" me (a play on the word cane) and why?—'cos . . . you know why—I'm saved—I am in the Mission for Jesus Christ, and I pray to Him and He helps me! You can come! We want you to come! Sam (turning to a particular boy chum with just as much show of feeling as a boy might risk in a company largely made up of boys), Sam, I do wish you would come—God can do for you the werry [sic] thing He's done for me.*

Such testimonies uttered in evident sincerity usually produced a marked effect upon the boys. The girls were more influenced by the girls, who, though often very shy, were generally more emotional and sometimes wonderfully eloquent with the un-trained eloquence of the heart. I have more than once seen a wholly unruly audience of two or three hundred children subdued to tears by the simple story of a girl's struggle for her mother's Salvation—*told by the child herself.*

In these Missions both in Whitechapel, and, as the work spread, at Three Coats Lane, in Bethnal Green and in Cambridge Heath, we suffered much open and violent opposition. I have now and again been with Rapson and a few of the saved boys and girls held prisoner for hours at a stretch, it being impossible to escape.

Cheap fireworks were freely used to annoy, and "stinkers" made from a mixture of common treacle, red pepper, and paraffin, which burned slowly and suffocatingly, were constantly in evidence! Tin whistles and broken tea trays sometimes produced a kind of pandemonium, while every type of East End fun was freely indulged in. But the work went on and proved the parent of much that followed. Numbers of children were undoubtedly saved, some of whom died in triumph, while others lived to fight as Salvation Soldiers in the days which then were far ahead.

The advance of the work to many aspects of the adult activities brought to the front more and more children, and questions arose as to the wisdom of allowing them to take part in the Meetings other than for children. Many of the boys especially developed striking gifts, and we began to use some of them in the adult Meetings—they spoke and sang and fished with much acceptance. Here were new dangers—very real dangers. But we had always a warning before us, and though the use of children in this way—that is, apart from their own Meetings—died down considerably as their own work extended and was better organized, I do not think this was because any very real harm had come of it. With regard to this aspect of the matter and the danger for children, especially the danger of their losing the simplicity of children, the Army Mother said at a Council in 1884: "Now directly a boy or girl leaves off being simple, he or she leaves off being a child, and becomes a sort of mixture between a grown-up person and an imp." There were, perhaps a few of these strange "mixtures" to be found amongst us—but never very many.

It was in the year 1881 that *"The Young Soldier,"* at first called *"The Little Soldier,"* was launched. It was a weekly paper and proved an immediate success. It has been of incalculable service to this work and of immense help also to many people outside our ranks who love the children and desire to bring them to Christ. It publishes freely communications from our Young People and, with its daughters in other lands, is probably the only newspaper in existence which can be placed in the hands of a child anxious about its own Salvation with any prospect of leading it to Christ.

In all the activities and organizing of those early days, rough and rollicking as they often were, there was kept steadily in view the original idea—carrying on *work for the Salvation of the childen by the children themselves.* Thus, as with the adult, or, as it has come to be called, the Senior work, it was *the creation of an organized force* which was aimed at. Just as we wanted an Army of Salvation among the grown-up people, so we wanted an Army of Salvation among the children. Such an Army must, of course, have serious limitations, as for example, in always losing its Soldiers to become Senior Soldiers as soon as they reach the age of maturity, and again, because its Recruits—Junior Soldiers as we call them—cannot be as fully under our direction as the Seniors, owing, for one thing, to the influence and control of their parents. Nevertheless, it was *an Army* we set out to raise, possessed of the same overruling spirit and purpose as that among the Seniors. *I am afraid that this is sometimes lost sight of even to-day.* And yet any one who really studies (*how earnestly I wish that Officers would study The Army more*), any one who studies the work in this department must see at once how this thought runs through it all. The raising of an Army is, in fact, the idea which unites the various operations and brings them all into one harmonious whole having one great aim.

The saved children—duly registered and cared for as such—are encouraged to testify to what God has done for them; they are urged to win their brothers and sisters and schoolfellows to Christ. Yes, and their parents also. They are to conduct their own Open-Air Meetings (I was so pleased to find from an Officer home on furlough in New Zealand that this is already seen in some Corps in China), and these Open-Airs were and are sometimes held in the face of much opposition and derision. The children are encouraged to speak of themselves as Junior Soldiers. They hold their own Meetings for prayer (I have heard lately of more than one blessed awakening which began with Children's Prayer Meetings—in one case it was prayer for the Salvation of their own parents); they sell *"The Young Soldier"* (I fear that this is not as frequent as it once was); they are encouraged to wear uniform (and warned against wearing showy or worldly clothes), urged to join the Young People's Bands or Singing Companies, and to play and sing for God. The elder ones are given Companies as soon as possible; they are encouraged to become Corps Cadets training for future work in The Army, and to make public confession of their intention to consecrate their lives as Officers—sometimes for service in the heathen lands.

All this and much more which is seen amongst us points to an organized force deliberately planned and led to aggressive work for God and man, and is as far as the east is from the west from a mere Sunday School or even from a special Service Mission.

I am deeply anxious that this work should continue to have the right direction. As to the outside children, we are in danger of overdoing what might be called the educational side of our efforts. It is, no doubt, good to teach them the truths which the Word of God declares, but if we stop there we have done but little for them! Their Salvation, *while children,* is to be our first great aim. What is the good of Bible reading, apart from Bible obedience; of observing Sunday if we profane the week-days? What, indeed, is the use of any teaching which does not in fact change and exalt the life and make it a life after Christ's own pattern and spirit? And how can this be done, whether in full-grown men or in children, without the New Birth and the New Creation which come by faith in Him? We know very well that it cannot be done. *We must go on*

73

to Salvation. That is our own proper work; that is the reason for our existence. *If we fail there we fail altogether!* Alas! is it not true that in some places we *have* failed? Have we not to bear the pain of seeing many children for whom we have laboured drift away from us and from God? Is there not in this a ground for grave concern, a call for close examination of our methods? In such cases ought there not at least to be at once a new beginning in determined and unsparing effort to bring the children to Christ?

And equally I wish our leaders to keep well before them that our aim continues to be, and must be, *the raising and maintaining of an organized force for God among the children.* The objective remains ever the same. *The children are called to be saved, and are chosen to fight and, if needs be, suffer, in order to win their fellows to Christ.*

Yes—to suffer! Just as many of the children in the early days of Christianity fought and witnessed and died for their testimony, so our children are to be led and trained to expect and to face opposition, whether in the form of ridicule at school or hatred at home, or of even more active persecution. Let us help them. Let us inspire them. Let us unite them. Let us lead them not merely to know the love and power of Christ Jesus in themselves, but to feel the burden of souls and to strive, in spite of suffering and distress, for their Salvation in their own simple, loving, trustful way.

CHAPTER EIGHT

Excerpts from:

"Of Such Is The Kingdom"

John Larsson

From The Salvation Army Year Book, 1980

Published by Salvationist Publishing and Supplies,
London

FOR an organization which takes its youth work as seriously as The Salvation Army does, it is surprising to find the centenary of the commencement of its youth operations falling a full 15 years after the centenary of the Army itself in 1965. Speaking in 1877 to the conference of The Christian Mission, William Booth had to admit:

"We have not as yet any real plan to propose for dealing with the children. So far as our experience of Sunday-schools has gone, they have been an injury to the Mission wherever they have existed. There are only three left, I believe." Then he added, "It must be distinctly understood that no new school must be commenced—in fact, no new plan of any kind must be adopted anywhere without my consent."

With this near embargo on children's work still in force The Christian Mission became The Salvation Army in 1878. It is idle to speculate on how long this restriction might have lasted, for in 1880 a seemingly unimportant event in the north of England altered the course of Army history.

Captain John Roberts, recently appointed to Blyth Corps, was having such a successful revival that children were being discouraged from attending in order to allow room for the crowds wanting to get in. One Sunday evening a little girl approached the Captain on his return from the open-air meeting. "Please, can I get into the meeting tonight?" she pleaded. "Certainly, if there is room," he replied. Immediately he felt the hollowness of his reply. He knew there would be no place for her.

Responding to what he was later to describe as a divine call, which in a flash revealed to him a great opportunity, there and then John Roberts decided to ignore the ban on new ventures and, without permission, called the child back and announced to her that there would be a children's meeting that Friday at 6 pm.

It was with some fear and trembling, he tells us, that he made his way to the hall that evening, but looking back on the occasion he could record: "A glorious time! About 70 present, and I was able to hold their complete attention for half an hour."

The date was Friday 30 July 1880, and the opening entry had been made in the history of Salvation Army youth work.

The work among children proved successful at Blyth and began spreading to neighbouring corps. Always ready to give his approval to what God seemed to be blessing, William Booth encouraged the new development. During the next few years the new emphasis on children's work began a southward march through England.

No master plan for the integration of young people's work within the corps structure had been thought out, but what developed was an amalgam of the well-known Sunday-school structure and a completely new concept: a Salvation Army corps *in miniature*. The "little" or junior soldiers were to have their own barracks, their own indoor and outdoor meetings, their own *junior* leaders (they were soon replaced by adults!). In fact, the "YP corps" was to be as faithful a small-scale replica of the real thing as could be devised, including the strong emphasis on a personal experience of salvation and training for evangelism and other service.

At the heart of the young people's corps programme was—and remains—the Sunday company meeting centered on teaching the Bible. To describe this as the Army's equivalent to Sunday-school would undoubtedly be correct, and yet it would be insufficient. With its stress on the need for personal commitment to Christ and training for service, the company meeting was meant to produce not so much scholars as soldiers. If the traditional Sunday-school resembled a day school, then the company meeting was more like a battle school.

Around the company meeting other aspects connected with the training and development of junior soldiers emerged, but it took 10 years and more of experimentation, change and adaptation before the kernel of the YP corps pattern as we know it today took form—and it needed strong administrative action to achieve that.

Despite amazing numerical advances—there were 18,000 junior soldiers by 1888, 744 YP corps, and *The Young Soldier* had a circulation of over 100,000—the "YP war" was still a patchy affair. "Field officers were under the impression that their interest in children was optional," comments Lieut-Commissioner Arch Wiggins. "Headquarters had to acknowledge that the junior soldiers' war had not been a success." It depended too much on the whims of individual officers. It was therefore decided to centralize operations and to control them from Headquarters as with the senior soldiers' war.

And so in August 1890—a quarter of a century after the Army's commencement on Mile End Waste—work among children was finally recognized administratively and was brought under the personal direction of divisional officers with divisional junior soldiers' secretaries being appointed to promote the work among the young.

Since 1890 the pattern of Army youth work has continued to develop and adapt itself to changing circumstances which include those of geography, for as the Army moved to other countries the basic YP corps concept had to be adapted to the special needs of each environment. The varieties of Army youth work around the world are therefore considerable, but all seek to work out in practice the stated aim of all Salvation Army youth work: "To bring young people to Jesus Christ and to develop them as fighting soldiers in the ranks of The Salvation Army."

And so by *some* steps—for not every corps has every step—or by all of them, the paths of the young people converge on that step where they are encouraged to assume adult Christian commitment as senior soldiers. The dominant aim of Army youth work is undoubtedly "to save"—the greatest gift that can be bestowed on a young person—and also to link with the Army as a place of service, a point the *Orders and Regulations* make clear: "The YP work will be judged successful inasmuch as it produces, in due course, senior soldiers who are truly converted, well acquainted with the Scriptures, imbued with the principles of The Salvation Army and zealous fighters for God."

The Salvation Army YP corps offers a comprehensive pattern of complementary programmes. The key element to its success is the availability of dedicated leaders, for the Army relies almost entirely on voluntary youth leaders. But if one adds to the corps structure the divisional and territorial superstructure of events, councils, weekend residential occasions for young people and training courses for their leaders, summer camps and schools, provision of material and an administrative and support structure with many full-time officers, there can be little doubt that the Army has come a long way since that day in 1877 when William Booth had to confess that there was "as yet no real plan" for dealing with the children. Could John Roberts have guessed that his response to a chance inquiry by a little girl would have led to all of this?

CHAPTER NINE

"Begin With The Children"

Cyril Barnes

From "Words Of Catherine Booth"

*Published by Salvationist Publishing and Supplies,
London 1981*

I WAS so glad to hear you had such a good meeting on Easter Monday," wrote Catherine Booth to her son, Bramwell, in 1873. She was preaching in Portsmouth to congregations of 3,000 people, but found time to encourage her son in his work among children. Bramwell was 17 and had written to his mother reporting success and she replied with approval and the thought that she would like to have been there.

Bramwell's meeting in the Whitechapel hall, in which 60 boys and girls had "come forward," followed a meal, for 500, of large buns and "as much tea as each could drink."

The same day his father, William, had led an open-air meeting on Mile End Waste, where he "unfurled the Mission flag, which bore the words, "We preach Christ and Him crucified" (possibly a banner or streamer). His service had attracted crowds, while only 20 people listened to a scoffing band of infidels holding a meeting close by. This was followed by a tea for 600 adults and a public meeting.

Mrs. Booth's letter also expressed the feeling that for William it was "a shame he should be so confined to the East End when the world is wanting him." Ten years later his world was 15 countries wide.

Catherine wanted Bramwell to develop as a public speaker. She felt sure it was his vocation. She pointed out its value: "If you *begin with the children* you will gain self-possession. You see you can talk to 300 or 400 in the same time and nearly as easily as you can talk to one, and always with more effect in the form of an address." All this was included in the letter of congratulation.

Bramwell had never been afraid to make his Christian witness. When only 13 years of age, he went to Tunbridge Wells for a holiday at the home of Henry Reed, a wealthy sheep-farmer returned from Tasmania. The visitor recorded his impressions on a now much-faded piece of paper. Everybody, he claimed, was very kind, but his greatest joy was that he "talked with Arthur very much and he seemed affected."

A few weeks later Bramwell, with brother Ballington and two of his sisters, attended a children's meeting at Bethnal Green. He gave his testimony, "I love Jesus," then stated: "I have never been to any of these meetings before, but I am very glad that I came tonight, and I think I shall come again. I want some of you—all of you—to give your hearts to God."

Bramwell went again and, encouraged by James Rapson, "who had a great gift for influencing children," was soon assisting him with the leadership. The meetings were held in a kitchen beneath the mission hall while adults were worshipping above. Bramwell recalled 60 years later that the room was infested with rats which he had to drive away without the children seeing or even knowing about them.

Following a two-year illness, during which he studied the Bible seriously, he returned to his work among the young people and soon became known in the Booth household as "Commissioner of the Children's Mission."

Catherine was never happier than when knowing that her children were helping with the work of the Mission.

CHAPTER TEN

"Saving the Children"
Samuel Logan Brengle

From "The Soul Winner's Secret"

*Published by Salvationist Publishing and Supplies,
London 1903, with many reprints*

NOT only did Jesus say, "Suffer the little children to come unto Me, and forbid them not," but He gave to Peter the positive command, "Feed My lambs," and in this command laid a responsibility upon soul-winners for the children, "for of such is the kingdom of heaven." In no other field and among no other class can they work with such immediate success and such far-reaching results.

Children are not hard to reach with the gospel, if the soul-winner will be simple and use common sense in dealing with them. They are not hardened in sin, their consciences are tender, their hearts open, their minds receptive, their wills pliable, their faith simple; they are keenly alive to the love of Jesus, the glories of heaven, the terrors of hell, and the power and sufficiency of God. They learn readily to pray in faith about everything and to cast all their care upon God. No eyes are so keen as theirs to see the Light that lighteth every man; no hands are so ready to do His bidding; no feet so ready to run in His ways.

And yet effort must be put forth ceaselessly to win them, and keep them after they are won, for the corruption of their own natures, the evil example and teaching of a hostile world, and the vigilant and tireless efforts of the enemy of all souls will soon blind their eyes, and harden their hearts, and utterly ruin them, if they are not soon won to Jesus and filled with His love.

You may feel yourself unfitted for this task, but it is your business to fit yourself for it, if God has called you to be a worker for souls. The first thing necessary is to believe in the possibility of the conversion of the children; and certainly the plain teachings of Jesus, the examples found in the Bible, and the multitude of examples that anyone can see with his own eyes, if he will open them and look, ought to convince the most skeptical of this possibility.

The Lord spoke to Samuel almost from his babyhood and filled his heart and mouth with wisdom, so that none of his words fell to the ground. From a child God ordained Jeremiah to be a prophet unto the nations, and filled him with His Spirit; and if this was possible under the law, how much more gloriously is it possible under the Gospel! Mrs. Catherine Booth was converted when but a child, the Army Founder when a mere lad, and all their sons and daughters were but children when they were brought to the Saviour.

Jonathan Edwards in one of his works tells of a wee girlie, only five years of age, going to and from her bedroom looking most sad and disconsolate. Her mother asked her what was the matter, and the little thing replied, "Mamma, when I pray God does not come." The mother tried to comfort her, but her little heart was filled with hunger which only the Comforter Himself could satisfy, and she still continued to go disconsolately to her bedroom. But one glad day she ran from her room, leaped into her mother's bosom, threw her arms around her mother's neck, and cried, "O Mamma, Mamma, when I pray now, God comes!" And up through the years of her childhood and youth and womanhood she lived such a life of Christlike humility and grace and truth as was the wonder of all who knew her.

Second, since they can be won, you must make up your mind that you *will* win them; but before this can be done you must put away from your mind for ever the idea that "anything will do for the children." It will require much prayer, and patience, and love, and tact, and divine wisdom to win them to the Saviour, and keep them after they are won. They must have "line upon line, precept upon precept." If one teaching of the lesson is not sufficient, then they must be taught it again and yet again and again. "Why do you tell Charles a thing twenty times over?" asked the father of John and Charles Wesley of the mother.

"Because nineteen times won't do," replied the wise and patient mother.

"Hear, O Israel," said the Lord: "The Lord our God is one Lord: and thou shalt love the Lord thy God with all thine heart, and with all thy soul, and with all thy might. And these words, which I command thee this day, shall be in thine heart: and thou shalt teach them diligently unto thy children, and shalt talk of them when thou sittest in thine house, and when thou walkest by the way, and when thou liest down, and when thou risest up. And thou shalt bind them for a sign upon thine hand, and they shall be as frontlets between thine eyes. And thou shalt write them upon the posts of thy house, and on thy gates" (Deut. vi. 4-9). This was the way that the children of the old Israelites were to be taught; and this must be the standard which the soul-winner sets for himself and for his people to-day.

The children should be noticed, and I am increasingly convinced that in every meeting where there are children present something should be said that is suitable to them, and the invitation to come to Jesus should include them.

When they do come, they should be dealt with most thoroughly: their little hearts should be probed, their sins searched out, and thorough repentance required. Their fears must be tenderly removed by showing them the fulness of God's love, and the certainty of salvation when they give up sin. Their thoughts should be turned to Jesus, and their faith fixed in Him and grounded in His word. Give them His sure promises, such as, "If we confess our sins, He is faithful and just to forgive us our sins, and to cleanse us from all unrighteousness" (I John i. 9). Above all, you must be simple and make things very plain for the children. They don't know the meaning of many big words that you understand quite well, therefore you must take pains to be simple and to make yourself understood.

The other day I was talking to some children, and I gave them this text: "Remember now thy Creator in the days of thy youth" (Eccl. xii. 1). I asked them if they knew what the word "Creator" meant, and none of them knew, neither did any of them know what the word "youth" meant. So I had to explain that the text meant that they were to remember and think about God, and love Him while they were little boys and girls.

Again, I gave them the text, "Behold, how good and how pleasant it is for brethren to dwell together in unity" (Ps. cxxxiii. 1), but none of them knew the meaning of the word "unity." One said that it meant "home," and that was a pretty good guess, but I had to explain that the text meant that it was good and pleasant for little brothers and sisters, and big ones, too, to live together in peace without quarrelling and fighting; and they all understood that.

You will have to put on your thinking caps, and set your brains to work to make your teaching simple for the children; but love will help you.

Some time ago I heard a youth worker singing lustily to a lot of children:

> Get your baggage on the deck,
> And don't forget to get your check,

..., but he didn't explain that it simply meant that they were to give themselves to Jesus, and throw away their sins, and be sure and get His love in their hearts. So when he got through I felt sure that nothing but a confused rattle of "baggage, deck, check, quick" remained in the ears of the children, with no useful or saving idea in their little heads and hearts.

If you pray to God for wisdom and love, He will help you to make the deepest spiritual truths plain to the children. As I simplify my talks God gives me the joy of seeing many young people seeking Him for salvation, and occasionally I have seen some gloriously sanctified.

Some time ago, in one of my meetings, I had a Penitent-form full of children, with each of whom I spoke personally. I asked one little fellow:

"What are you here for?"

"To get saved," said he.

"To get saved from what? I inquired.

"From my sins."

"And what are your sins?"

"I fight," and then he broke down and cried.

"And what are you here for?" I asked a little girl.

She, too, said she was there to get saved, and I asked her what her sins were. She hesitated a little and then said, "I'm cruel to my little brothers and sisters;" and then she, too, broke down and cried.

Another little girl said that she swore, and another that she disobeyed her mother. One little boy confessed that he told lies; another, that he smoked cigarettes; and another, that he was disobedient to his teacher. And so they told of their sins, and broke down and wept and prayed, and asked God to forgive them, and I believe that most of them got saved.

In another meeting a little fellow of ten got sanctified and filled with the Spirit, and had all fear taken out of his heart, where before he had been very timid. "Because," said he, "Jesus is with me now." In yet another meeting a little girl, about ten years of age, got sanctified. She lived a holy life for about three years, and then died happy, sending me word that the Lord still sanctified her and kept her to the end.

But after we have done all, we must remember that they are only lambs, not sheep; that they are growing children, not grown men and women; that they are in the formative state; that they are tender and inexperienced; that life and the world are full of interest to them; that they have a personality and individuality of their own; that they are not always willing to take a simple word of their elders, nor to yield to admonition and instruction, but desire to prove their own power, and to "taste and see" all things for themselves. Therefore it will be necessary, not only to talk much to them about God, but to talk even more to God about them, and to depend upon the mighty and constant cooperation of the Holy Spirit in securing their salvation and keeping them in the grace of our Lord Jesus Christ.

We must show all diligence in our efforts until, if possible, we can at least say with Paul to Timothy, that "from a child thou hast known the Holy Scriptures, which are able to make thee wise unto salvation through faith which is in Christ Jesus" (2 Tim. iii. 15).

Blessed Jesus, *save* our children!
  Be their Guardian through life's way;
From all evil e'er protect them,
  Walk Thou with them, come what may.
In white raiment let us meet them
  When earth's shadows flee away.

Blessed Jesus, *lead* our children
  Into paths of service sweet:
Up the hill of Calvary climbing,
  May they and the sinner meet!
More than conquerors, let us see them
  Bring their jewels to Thy feet!

Blessed Jesus, *make* our children
  Thine for life and Thine for aye!
When death's waters overtake them,
  Be their Rock, their Light, their Stay!
Tender Shepherd, let us find them
  On Thy breast in realms of day!

Rough and ready Peter, that horny-handed fisherman, thought he was cut out for and best fitted to be a prime minister or secretary of state or a bishop, and, it seems, had several disputes with the other disciples as to whether he should not be the greatest among them. How intense must have been his surprise, then, when he got his commission from Jesus as a young-people's worker, and received orders to feed the lambs! What a mighty argument he could have made to prove that he was not fitted for work with the children! To be sure, he had at least one boy of his own, and maybe several others; but then, he was a fisherman, and the care of the children was very largely left to his wife. In fact, he had no fitness either by nature or by training for that kind of work; all his associations had been with the big, burly men of the sea, and what did he know about talking to children? All his thoughts and desires and ambitions ran in another direction, and was he not too old and set in his ways to change now?

But when Jesus, with infinite knowledge and wisdom and tenderness, looked straight into his eyes, and asked him that searching question, "Lovest thou Me more than these?" and then in reply to his answer, "Yea, Lord, Thou knowest that I love Thee," said, "Feed My lambs" (John xxi. 15), what could Peter reply? So Peter was first commissioned to be a worker among the little ones.

"But," you say, "did not Jesus mean young converts when He said, "My lambs"? and might they not be men and women who were only newly converted?" True, it is probable that Jesus meant new converts, but new converts include children, for the children are often converted too, and did not Jesus say, with reference to the children, "of such is the kingdom of God"? (Luke xviii. 16). So, however we may explain the text, we cannot get away from the fact that Peter was commanded to work with and for the children. And if Peter, why not you and I? Are we not commanded to look well to the flock over which the Holy Ghost hath made us overseers? and was there ever a flock in which there were no lambs? If so, it was a flock doomed to speedy extinction.

Are we not commanded to do with our might what our hands find to do? And do we not find multitudes of little ones unshepherded, unloved, and untaught, for whose tender little souls no man cares, nor prays, nor weeps before the Lord, and whose little hands are stretched out toward us, saying, "Come and help us"? Shall we wait till they are old in sin and hardened in wickedness and fixed in unholy habits, and bond-slaves of the devil, before we work and plan and pray for them and seek their salvation?

Is it possible that we have a call to the work of saving souls, and yet have no commission for the children? No, no, no! To everyone who says to Jesus, "Lord, Thou knowest that I love Thee," in answer to His question, "Lovest thou Me?" Jesus says, "Feed My lambs." A man may feel that he has no fitness, no tact, no skill, no gifts for that kind of work, but the commission lays upon him the responsibility to study and think, and watch and pray, and love and believe, and work himself into fitness. By beginning with just such poor, feeble, untrained gifts as he has, by making the most of every opportunity, by being diligent and faithful, by courage, and pluck, and good cheer, and faith, and by seeking God's blessing day by day, he may surely attain this fitness.

The poor, besotted drunkard who never dreamed he had any music in his soul or in his fingers till he got converted at the Salvation Army Penitent-form, but who sets himself to it and patiently blows away at an instrument for six months until he can play fairly well, can with equal diligence and patience and determination and attention learn to interest and bless and help the children; but he must put his heart and soul into it.

I read some time since of a minister who was sure he was called and fitted only to preach big sermons to big folks, but one day he heard a brother minister talk so instructively and entertainingly to the children that he determined to acquire that gift, and by thought and prayer and practice he, too, became a powerful children's worker.

Go thou, my brother, my sister, and do likewise.

Do you ask, "How can I become such a worker?"

I. Make up your mind that you *ought* to do so, and that by God's grace you *will; then,* make it a matter of daily prayer and thought and meditation. Above all, seek help from God.

II. Get all the help you can from others. Study their methods, but do not become a vain imitator of anyone. Be yourself.

III. Study the best books you can find on the subject. There are many bright books that will greatly help you.

IV. Try to put yourself in the place of the child, and ask what would interest you. Make things very plain and simple. Watch for illustrations and anecdotes that the children can understand, and that will interest them.

V. But, above all, have a heart full of tender love and sympathy for the little ones, and you will be interesting and helpful to them whether you can talk much or not. They will feel your love and respond to it, and so you can point them to Jesus, and help them in their first timid steps toward heaven.

CHAPTER ELEVEN

"The Salvationist And Children"

John D. Waldron

From "The Army Bookshelf"

Published in The War Cry (U.S.A. Edition)
July 16, 1983

THE Army bookshelf is well stocked with publications about children and for children. The slogan "Every Child Matters" was not only the theme for an international campaign but is at the very heart of all the Army's endeavors.

It may be surprising, then, to discover that the first references to work among children are fragmentary. **Robert Sandall** describes (in *The History of The Salvation Army,* Volume I) the earliest children's meetings held at the Whitechapel Mission, where "many children came in from curiosity, frequently shoeless, bonnetless, ragged, and dirty in the extreme." The same volume tells of teenager Bramwell Booth assisting in Children's Mission meetings in Bethnal Green in 1869.

Colonel Sandall describes scattered efforts during subsequent years, but in 1877 it was largely abandoned, since "it had become apparent that this great work could not be carried on efficiently without a separate organization under leaders willing to devote themselves to the children . . . only the slow process of years could produce the necessary staff."

The personal interest of the Booths in children, however, is well documented. In 1884 **William Booth** published *The Training of Children*. Modern parents and youth workers might consider some parts of this book to be dated. However, it contains some very choice chapters of sound advice on the responsibility of parents, reading, companionships, health, the training of "little soldiers" and many other subjects. Fortunately, this classic was reprinted in 1976 and is worth exploring.

In that delightful book, *Sergeant-Major Do-Your-Best*, the Founder has a chapter on "A Lover of the Juniors" in which he describes the attitudes of Captain Highflyer, Captain Tall-Talk and Captain Bigheart towards children's work. Reprinted in 1981, it is now available to all Salvationists, and its "Sketches of the Inner Life of the Salvation Army Corps" combines humor, pathos and common sense. Catherine Booth's interest in Bramwell's children's meetings is described in **Cyril Barnes'** book, *Words of Catherine Booth*, under the appropriate title, "Begin with the Children." **Emma Booth-Tucker** has a moving chapter on "Save the Children" in her book, *The Cross Our Comfort*, unfortunately now out of print.

As **Bramwell Booth** pointed out in a Staff Review article describing the early-day children's meetings, "The work of the Army for the salvation of children really began in the home of the Founders." The genesis of the modern day children's work, however, is described in the book *John Roberts, Evangelist,* by his daughter **Ethel B. Rohu.** General Albert Orsborn, in his foreword, writes, "I commend to Salvationists and Christian friends everywhere this well-told story of the man who, in an inspired moment, began to hold Salvation Army meetings for children in Blyth on Friday, July 30, 1880."

By all means, read this book with its story of Minnie Brownell and the overcrowded hall, the "manifesto" of John Roberts, and the General's decision that "these meetings must be started all over the country."

Thus was born the worldwide ministry of the Army among children, taking more forms than could be described in a score of books. Something of the scope of its development, but still far from exhaustive, is described by **John Larsson** in the *1980 Year Book* under the title "Of Such Is the Kingdom."

Many of yesterday's youth leaders were inspired by a book from the pen of the delightful **Catherine Baird,** onetime editor of the American *Young Soldier.* Also entitled *Of Such Is the Kingdom,* she writes about "The Core of our Message," "A Resourceful Teacher," "The Child in the Temple" and other subjects. Her words are marked by a love for children which certainly must always be our central characteristic.

Samuel Logan Brengle was well known for his love of children. In his book, *The Soul Winner's Secret,* he devotes two chapters to the theme, "Saving the Children." His concluding paragraphs answer the question, "How can I become an effective children's worker?" In brief, he suggests five points: "Make up your mind that you ought to do so, and that by God's grace you will; get all the help you can from others; study the best books you can find on the subject; try to put yourself in the place of the child; above all, have a heart full of tender love and sympathy for the little ones."

As Brengle points out in his essay "They Are Only Lambs," reprinted in the book *At the Center of the Circle,* "The children should be noticed...you must take pains to make yourself understood."

Today's authors continue the tradition, and lists of current Army books about children and for children can be secured from your territorial youth secretary. For example, in *Encounter,* **Anita Phillipson Robb** has a series of choice vignettes under the heading "Every Child Matters." A new book by **J. Gordon Wilder** tells a fascinating story in *Rufus T. Spooner and the Life-Saving Scouts*. Some delightful books are being published for the children themselves. And the older generation will respond to **Flora Larsson's** chapter entitled "Confessions of a Grandma" in her book *From My Treasure Chest*.

Yes, the patter of little feet can be heard running up and down the Army bookshelf, emphasizing the fact that to the Salvationist, every child really does matter.

CHAPTER TWELVE

"Every Child Matters"

Anita Phillipson Robb

From "Encounter"

*Published by The Salvation Army
Eastern Territory, New York 1982*

Baby in a Box

THAT baby has to be God's child," said the dispatcher of Salvation Army dropbox crews from the Army's Adult Rehabilitation Center. He was talking about a newborn baby boy pulled out of one of the dropboxes which are intended to receive usable soft goods. Such boxes are emptied on a prearranged schedule.

On a particularly cold winter's day, the crew had passed up the city where the dropbox was located because their truck was already overloaded. Instead of skipping a day to return on their regular schedule, the crew continued their usual route the following morning, and came back to the dropbox they had missed on the previous day. As the men on the truck cleared out the dropbox and handed up the packages to the driver, the latter heard a noise as he stacked the boxes. "I thought it was another kitten," he said; "people are always putting them into the boxes."

In spite of the difficulty of searching for anything in a load of toys, furniture, clothing, magazines, and newspapers, the driver, with his two helpers, stopped their work and began to search for the source of the noise on the truck. It was not long before the driver found a shopping bag which he handed to one of his helpers. The man pulled aside a blanket and found a baby boy almost blue with cold, and obviously, very new.

Closing the bag, the men swiftly moved to the cab of the truck and turned on the engine to warm the baby, while one of the men went to call the police. "Nothing like that ever happened to me before," said the truck driver, "and I hope it never does again. If we hadn't found that little fellow when we did, he would have frozen to death."

When the police arrived, the four-pound-11-ounce, blue-eyed baby was taken to a nearby hospital and placed in an incubator, while police began the search for his mother. It was felt that the blanket with a distinctive design, which had been wrapped around the infant, would be a leading clue to the mother.

"If the baby had not cried when he did, he would probably have been suffocated," said the dispatcher. And the men in the truck added, "We feel real good about the whole thing, and we're sure glad that we had that overload yesterday."

It is hard to understand why a mother would abandon her helpless baby, but God in His providence overrules man. If the pickup had been made on schedule, the baby would have been in the box for two days instead of a few hours. The clothing tossed on top of the tiny boy helped to insulate him from the cold. Crying when he did saved him from suffocation under a truckload of donated used clothing and other articles.

The good news that someone cares and will help persons in need has to be continually broadcast, so that all may know that they need not use such desperate measures to try to solve their dilemmas.

Loved for Herself

Ruth Ann's mother took one look at her newborn armless child and walked out of the hospital, leaving Ruth Ann behind. The child remained there for the next four years. Since she had no arms, Ruth Ann did not learn to walk because she could not balance herself. Fortunately, when she was four years old, she was placed with the Salvation Army Foster Home Service where a worker found a suitable home for her.

The famed Dr. Howard Rusk, pioneer in rehabilitation, took a personal interest in developing the proper prosthesis for Ruth Ann. This made it possible for the little girl to learn to walk and to do things for herself with her new hands.

Ruth Ann developed into a beautiful preteen girl who is loved for herself and who loves others in return. She enjoys dancing and does all of the things most normal 12-year-olds usually enjoy.

Loving foster parents and the proper medical attention have helped to turn Ruth Ann's potentially disastrous life into one of joy and great potential for the future.

Neglected and Rejected

Sixteen-year-old Terri wanted a "mama" and it was beyond her comprehension to understand why her natural mother did not want her. She had never known who her father was.

Terri's mother, an alcoholic who supported herself and her habit through association with a variety of men friends, pushed her only child out of the house. For a number of months, Terri lived with any of her friends or acquaintances who would take her in. When she became pregnant, Terri went home to ask her mother for help. Instead of giving it, her mother called the police and preferred delinquency charges against her daughter. When the true situation became known, the mother was charged with neglect and Terri was made a ward of the court.

Terri was given intensive psychotherapy and counseling at the Salvation Army maternity home to which she had been referred by a probation officer. The young girl felt utterly abandoned, and no amount of help could persuade her that foster home placement with her baby, which she had chosen to keep and could do so legally, would solve her problems.

It is problems such as Terri's that Salvation Army officers and other professional workers face daily: how can a sixteen-year-old who desperately loves a mother who has rejected her become an emotionally stable, mature mother to her own baby? Those working with Terri hope to help her to reach that goal.

A Divided Life

The police brought 14-year-old Ann, disheveled, without shoes, and nearly hysterical, to The Salvation Army's Runaway House.

Ann had started to hitchhike to Florida with a young man whom she had met when she ran away from the boarding school in which her divorced parents had placed her. Enroute, the two hitchhikers were invited to a party which turned out to be a sordid affair. While she was defending herself, Ann's glasses were knocked off, sending her into a great panic since she could not see without them. After being raped several times, Ann managed to run out of the house screaming for help. The police, responding to a neighbor's call, took Ann to Runaway House.

Ann was a beautiful teenager with great potential, but with strong feelings of rejection by her parents. After a few days, however, she was able to call her mother, who worked as a cocktail hostess in a southern city. Her mother promised to send for her.

Not long after that, Ann's father, a successful businessman living abroad, came to Runaway House. He did not greet his daughter with any expression of concern about her horrifying experience, nor did he show her any affection. His first comment was, "What are we to do with you?"

After providing money and clothes for Ann, he took her home to her mother—a doubtful solution for the young girl's problems.

Culture Shock

Dragging your daughter down the street by her long hair may be acceptable practice in some countries but not in the United States. Kim, a 17-year-old high school senior, had incurred the wrath of her businessman father when he learned that she had been dating one of her high school classmates, while steadfastly refusing to marry an older man with whom her father had made a marriage arrangement for her.

Called by neighbors who had witnessed the scene, police arrived to find Kim cowering before her father who brandished a gun and threatened his daughter in an old-world fashion. Fearing for her safety, police removed Kim from the home and took her to the Salvation Army Girls' Hostel where she spent six weeks while the courts tried to decide her future.

Lieutenant June, who was on the early morning shift at the hostel, used the extended quiet time before breakfast to read her Bible and have her personal devotions. Unknown to the Lieutenant, Kim had been observing her at devotions for some time. Then one morning Kim asked the Lieutenant what she was reading. Quietly, Lieutenant June explained the purpose of her devotions in terms of Kim's own religious upbringing. The Bible fascinated the young girl, and she asked if she could have a copy to read. From then on, Kim avidly read her "new book" at every opportunity.

The court finally decided to offer Kim the opportunity to live in a foster home while she completed high school and reached 18 years of age. This young girl had begun to absorb the message of the New Testament which she had been reading over and over. Weighing her family's customs against what she had been reading, Kim's decision was to go home.

It was a difficult decision for Kim to make since the only person in her family who would speak to her was her mother. Her father banished Kim from her formerly pleasant room to a cramped space in the basement, and she was required to remain there. Except for school, no other activities were permitted, nor was Kim allowed to communicate with anyone in the family, by order of her unforgiving father.

Kim accepted all of these changes with good grace. She occasionally called the Lieutenant from school to thank her for her beloved Bible which she had somehow been able to keep and which, she said, gave her strength to face her situation.

Damaged But Not Destroyed

It seems almost beyond belief that Cindy had spent eleven years of her young life confined to the furnace room of her home. Neither the heat from the furnace nor the scraps from the family table did anything to warm or feed her body and certainly did not satisfy the hunger of her empty heart.

Cindy was eventually discovered by the authorities and was sent to the Salvation Army Children's Village. It was not easy to communicate with this child who had been robbed of personal growth through lack of human relationships. Learning to trust adults was not easy for Cindy and the freedom to move about was frightening to her.

Slowly the warmth of God's love, expressed through caring staff members, began to penetrate the walls of Cindy's loneliness and fear. It was a learning and growing process which developed little by little as she tested, tried, and triumphed in her new life. As her self-confidence increased, Cindy's awareness of the resources available to her made it possible for her to step out of her teens into an adult world. It was good to know that although that adult world had damaged her, it had not destroyed her.

Cindy learned about God's love through the lives of those around her and, as she attended services at the corps, she eventually trusted her life to Christ who had said so lovingly: *"Suffer the children to come unto Me."*

Just Like You!

Six-year-old Michael was indeed fortunate when the court removed him and his 14-year-old sister from their home. Michael was sent to the Salvation Army Children's Village, and Grace went to live with an older sister. The court acted because of their father's prolonged absence, and their alcoholic mother's inability to function as a parent.

The village with its family cottages, plentiful activities, and loving staff members soon helped Michael to experience a happier life. Grace visited him every week and longed to be a part of the village. She was finally able to persuade her public agency caseworker that such a change would be in her best interest. Grace reported to her worker that men came to see her sister and that she did not want to grow up to be like that sister.

The village provided opportunity for life experiences which neither Michael nor Grace had ever known nor could ever have experienced within their own family circle. Taking advantage of the educational opportunities offered her, Grace became a registered nurse.

Her happy marriage to a man of another faith proved to be entirely workable, for when the children came along he wanted them to be baptized in Grace's church. "I want our children to be just like you," was her husband's warm, admiring statement.

Too Ugly to Handle!

Dave was crushed and bitter when he had no alternative but to bring his son to the Salvation Army Children's Treatment Center for help. His boy was stealing, fighting, a truant from school, and generally out of parental control.

This seemed to Dave to be a replay of his own life. His memory forced him to deal with feelings too ugly to handle, too conflict-ridden to understand, and too personal to expose.

Dave's teen years had also been spent in a children's institution. His ugly behavior, the only expression he had had for feelings of anger and hurt, could not be tolerated by those responsible for him. He was placed in a "home for bad boys," where he had been locked into a system that manipulated behavior and misinterpreted feelings.

Dave's life became a parade of antisocial behavior. His way of living led him to drink, to jail, to an early marriage, to early parenthood, to separation, to psychiatric services, to Alcoholics Anonymous and, finally, with his son, to the office of a Salvation Army treatment center where he was able to tell how helpless he felt when he saw the pattern of his own life unfolding in his son's behavior. Dave felt that he was committing his son to the same destructive path that he had experienced. The difference lay in the fact that the children's institutions today care about the "good" in the child, and they also care about the "good" in a parent.

After long months of counseling at the children's center from which his son had been discharged much earlier, Dave found security and fellowship when, at an Army meeting, he placed his life in Christ's control. A new life in Christ, and ongoing supportive counseling, has compelled Dave to understand that Christ, although Himself rejected, does not reject those who turn to Him.

The Scapegoat

Fifteen-year-old Sandra, the middle child of three, had become the family scapegoat. Her harried businessman father commuted daily to his work in the city. In the evenings he tried to keep his family together, following the death of his wife two years earlier.

Sandra had a poor self-image, was average in school, had rowdy friends, and occasionally drank a little. She was a very pretty girl but felt completely rejected by her sisters. Her father disciplined her, but she always felt that he did not support her in anything she tried to do. Fortunately a street worker knew where to send Sandra when she finally split from her family and had no place to go. The Salvation Army's New-Life House became a place of new beginnings for all of the family.

After a few quiet days and some counseling, Sandra consented to meet with her father and a counselor. Prior telephone conferences by the staff worker had not been profitable as Sandra's father would not accept any responsibility for her behavior.

The conference between parent and child was highly charged emotionally. It did make it possible, however, for Sandra's father to admit that he may have been wrong in his judgments and to tell

Sandra that he really did love her. She gained insights about her father's efforts to be both homemaker and breadwinner.

Sandra decided on her own that she would return home. Counseling was arranged so that problems would not pile up beyond a point of tolerance for her. That was some months ago and while the family still has its problems, they are no longer overwhelmed by them.

Friends at Last

Jennie was a beautiful black girl with high goals for herself and a willingness to work hard to achieve them. She was brought to the Salvation Army Runaway House because of her inability to cope with the continual strife between her mother and father.

Jennie's mother had reared her family with public assistance. She worked hard and admitted to cheating sometimes in order to send her older children to college. Jennie had also set college education as a goal, and she worked during the summer to help realize her ambition.

Her father had been in and out of the home when the children were young, but finally the parents had been divorced. Jennie's dad always insisted that she was not his child and refused to support her. Eventually he married again, succeeded in his business efforts, and enjoyed a comfortable home.

When Jennie was about 14 or 15, she and her alleged father became really acquainted. When he saw what a beautiful and talented girl Jennie had become, he offered her a home and advantages that her mother could not provide. Torn by her loyalty to her mother and tempted by the offered help from her father, Jennie chose to live and work with a foster family. She finally ran away and appeared at Runaway House.

Jennie had three weeks at Runaway House to sort out her

feelings and make some choices. She at last made a decision to go to her father where she has lived for the past year. She will soon be graduated from high school, and she is happy that at last she is friends with both of her parents.

Home Is a Haven

Winter had come early during that particular November, and the ground was covered with snow. In the big playground at the Salvation Army Children's Village, the snow had created strange-looking shapes which resembled monsters—at least the children thought so. One big open space held the footprints from the "fox-and-geese" game played there the previous afternoon.

Captain Mary, the administrator, usually had other things on her mind than viewing the playground in the early morning hours. But for some reason when the chimes rang for breakfast, she looked out of the window before leaving her room. To her astonishment, there stood a young boy beside his bicycle in a corner of the playground.

Putting on warm clothes, the Captain hurried to the boy and saw that it was Ricky M. who said he had "come home." A year or so earlier, Ricky had spent a number of happy months at the village.

His placement in a variety of earlier foster homes had left the little boy very confused, and Ricky had finally found stability at the Children's Village. Since small boys need regular parents, Ricky eventually was sent to another foster home. He had fled from this home, riding his bike across the city.

His simple statement to Captain Mary expressed his feelings clearly; "No one ever listened to me except at the village." Here he felt safe and knew that someone would always be willing to listen to anything he had to tell.

Not As Old As She Wanted To Be

Mrs. Janue worked full time to support 14-year-old Lucy and 17-year-old John. While Lucy and John had some home responsibilities, they both had too much unsupervised time.

Mrs. Janue had been married and divorced three times, and Lucy so heartily disliked her mother's current boyfriend that she decided to run away. Since Lucy's home was in a small midsouthern town, she was unprepared for the kind of life naive and unsophisticated girls so often experience in the city. She hitchhiked to a large metropolitan area where a motorcycle gang took her in.

One of the fellows, a 30-year-old, decided to go to Chicago with Lucy as a passenger. On arriving in the city he suddenly became ill, and the police took him to a hospital.

Lucy tried to convince the police that she was 20 years old, but it was easy to see that this was not true. As she later said, "They didn't buy it." The police took her to a Salvation Army group home for runaways.

After a few days in the home, where she had time to think things over, Lucy confided to the counselor that she was tired of lying but saw no solution to her problems. Fortunately for Lucy, her hometown had three counseling services, and the workers at one agreed to help the young girl and her mother. By this time Mrs. Janue was so distraught that she was willing to promise almost anything to get her daughter home again.

Learning to Accept Himself

When JD was four years old he was considered to be an autistic child because he shut himself away from communication with his family. That is never an easy situation for even stable parents to deal with, and this difficult child proved too much for his family to handle. He was removed from his neglectful and abusing parents and placed in a state facility for treatement.

Fortunately for JD, when he was 11 years old he became a resident of the Salvation Army Children's Village. There he was placed in a cottage family where he learned to cope with stress and to be accepted for himself.

As a young teenager, JD took part in a special training program on education for parenthood. The experience was like the opening of a door for him. Not only did his school work improve but his behavior stabilized. Part of the training program took place at a nearby daycare center. JD did so well and became so interested in the center program that he asked for and secured a job there during the summer.

JD feels much better about himself now and has developed a sense of self-worth. The child who seemed beyond the care of his parents is now able to care for others.

How It All Began—Salvation Army Services to Children

It all began in England in the mid-1880's when the need for the care of children outside of their homes was evident. William Booth was opposed to total care, having been influenced by the writings of Dickens about Victorian orphanages.

As soon as it became evident that more than temporary solutions were needed, the Booths clearly stated the principles governing the care of children in institutions. They should be the same as those a family uses in governing its children in the home. An early book, *The Training of Children,* or how to make the children into saints and soldiers of Jesus Christ, was written in a question-and-answer style.

The first question was: "What is the supreme duty of parents with regard to their children?" The answer: "The duty of parents to their children is to govern, influence, and inspire them that they love, serve, and enjoy God and, in consequence, grow to be good, holy, and useful men and women."

The Salvation Army has provided, and still provides, unique services for handicapped children in many countries where such children are often considered expendable. Some examples of the Army's concern are: Joytown for handicapped children in Africa; schools and workshops for the blind in several countries; institutions for the mentally retarded; children's homes for orphans or half-orphans, etc.

In the United States, the Army has some institutionally based programs for children who require this type of care. However, in this country, the emphasis is on the care of children in their homes. Through corps community centers a host of activities in recreation have been established: scouting, camping, musical groups, and other educational programs, as well as spiritual guidance through Sunday schools geared to meet children's needs.

The Army deeply feels that every child *does* matter and must be given protection as well as opportunity for development. Whatever form the service may take, the goal is the same: to provide an atmosphere in which a child may develop his fullest potential for self-realization and self-responsibility.

CHAPTER THIRTEEN

"A Lover of the Juniors"

William Booth

From "Sergeant-Major Do-Your-Best"

*Published by Salvationist Publishing and Supplies,
London 1906
Reprinted by Triumph Press, Toronto 1981*

NOW, there's one more thing about our Captain which I like, and I won't say any more after that, lest you should think I am partial, and have favourites, which I haven't, except it is for those who come up to my notions, which I have told you what they are, so that you can judge for yourself.

But there is one thing I do like our Captain for, and that is, he is a boy for the Juniors. Now, perhaps it is through Sarah drilling it into me at home that it's the children that makes the men and women Soldiers of a few years to come; and perhaps it is through thinking that I might have been a Captain myself, or perhaps a Divisional Officer, if there had been anybody to make me a Junior Soldier; or, perhaps it is through having seen the children of so many of my neighbours, and some of our Soldiers, grow up to be drunkards and ne'er-do-wells, for want of being taken hold of when they were young. I don't know, but I do believe in the Juniors, and I do want to see them done well for.

Then, perhaps it is because our Junior Corps has been so shamefully neglected for some years past by some of our Officers, that has made me think so much more of what our Captain has done for it.

There was Captain Highflyer. He told me himself that he was not going to spend his precious time, and his God-given abilities, on a lot of ignorant children. He had something more important to do. His mission was to their fathers and mothers: he would get them saved, and they must look after the children.

Then, there was Captain Mary Tall-Talk. Why, the first week she was here she met the Junior Locals, and addressed them for three-quarters of an hour about the importance of the children being saved, and about the way the thing should be done, and a great deal more, but she never lifted her little finger towards doing it. Bless her, she had a good deal to do, and worked very hard at it, but she did nothing for the children.

There was Captain Bigheart. He worked night and day, himself and his Lieutenant, and made quite a respectable thing of the children's meetings; but not having made a proper Junior Staff, and taught them how to keep our work going, it nearly all fell away when Bigheart left.

Now, our Captain, you see, goes into the work like business. He has fixed himself up at some of the meetings, and he takes his appointments like a machine. He examines the Junior Soldier Locals, visits the sick children, and loves and labours for the youngsters as conscientiously as he does for the Seniors.

And he has some blessed times with them, I can tell you. Why, there was dear little Patty Paleface, who was sick for six weeks. He visited her almost every day, and talked and sung to her, and took her nice little cups of milk stuff with his own hands, that his wife made for her. And when Patty died it was like Heaven to be in the chamber, and half the place came to the funeral, and he got her drunken father and backslidden mother both saved at the memorial service.

Yes, I like our Captain. Long may he live! I have only one regretful feeling about him, and that comes over me when I think of the day that he will be taken from our Corps. But God must have many more as good as he is in this blessed Army, for I thoroughly believe in our Officers.

Salvationist Poems About Children

Do the Children Cry?

Do the children cry?
Or do they lie silent—remote from life—
   with vacant, staring eyes?
Do they yearn for love, and dare to hope
   for comfort somewhere, somehow, in this stench of death?
Or has hope fled? Or never yet been born?

Dear God—these tiny, helpless ones!
Victims of unfathomable hate!

Dear God—the agony of motherhood!
To watch one's children die!

Take—take the love poured from my heart,
And carry it to Your benighted ones.
Accept my stumbling prayer, my deep concern,
A humble sharing in this urgency.

Hold—hold these dear ones in Your love,
And help them feel the tenderness, the strength.
Turn them to hope—to dare to look again
   forward, and up into Your thorn-scarred face.
Dear God—that they may weep, and laugh, and live again!

by Joan Corner
(Inspired by a "War Cry" descrip-
tion of scenes from Cambodia, from
the pen of Lt.-Colonel John Bate)

There He Stood Amid a Crowd

There He stood among a crowd:
   Who was He, and who were they?
He was Jesus, Son of God,
   They were children at their play.

Now He called them unto Him,
   Round they gathered, full of glee;
Some were standing by His side,
   Others seated on His knee.

His disciples, too, were there;
   Master, Thou are tired, said they,
Children will disturb Thee here,
   Let us send them all away.

Let them stay, the Master said,
   They are very dear to Me;
Then upon each little head
   Laid His hands so tenderly.

Look at them and learn to be
   Lowly, meek, and free from care;
Suffer them to come to Me,
   Such shall in My kingdom share.

Kitty Wood

131

Across the Street

"PLEASE Miss," she said (her voice was sweet),
Do take my hand across the street."
And I, from lofty five foot four,
Looked down, She was but five, not more—
A cap of blue, a coat all torn,
Two little shoes, both scuffed and worn,
A dirty smudge upon her nose,
Brown eyes—they were not meant for prose!

I took her clinging hand in mine,
'Twas raining, yet I saw stars shine
As, glad, I led those baby feet
Across the busy, crowded street,
And while I watched her smallness race
Away, my thoughts began to chase
The brown eyes and the wee smudged nose,
Till from my soul a prayer arose:

LORD, in Thy mercy and good grace,
If we've grown tall, and if our pace
Is sure and strong, as through our days
We, fearless, move through life's strange maze,
Grant us to heed the plaintive tone
Of little ones, who've not yet grown
In wisdom. Let us guide their feet,
As through a busy, crowded street.
Nor pride ourselves, because we know

The truth it pleaseth Thee to show
To us Thy children in the street,
For once we moved with faltering feet.
So, woe to us, if ill betide
Them while they're walking by our side,
Or if we lead their steps astray
Instead of by the Living Way.

by Catherine Baird

Children

When I see the children,
Innocent and pure,
I'm lost in wonder
That You can endure
The thought of what
They may in fact become
Before the long race
Of their life is run.
Their predecessors
Give You endless pain,
And yet You have the heart
To try again!

It's true they give Your kindness
Lots of scope,
And prove to me
You still believe
In hope!

John Gowans

133

Growing Pains

Growing pains are real, Lord!
People may regard them as an old wives' tale,
   but they are stark reality;
at any rate in teenage thinking and feeling
   if not in an actual physical sense.

Growing up is painful, Master.
It is a comfort to know that You too
passed through the restless adolescent years,
though that was in a quiet country town
and not in the hurly-burly of modern life
   dominated by TV and radio.

To realize who one is, what one is,
   to be aware of deep new urges
   and awesome possibilities ...
It's quite frightening, Lord!
The tension between childhood and adulthood
   is pendulum-like in its movement;
one day one thing, the next another.

Be my anchor, Master! Hold me fast
even when I sway between conflicting loyalties
and swing and swoop in changing moods.
Keep me on a steady keel,
   a steady spiritual keel,
until the turbulence of the growing years subsides.
Keep my heart centered on Yourself
   until these temporary storms are over
and I enter adulthood's comparative calm.

Flora Larsson

The Toddler

I am youth winding up,
Like a top,
Eating excitement as mashed
Potatoes,
Chomping curiosity as
Peanut brittle.
I am a pusher and a puller,
And even bite if confused
Or angry or pained.
I am youth newly leaped
From the mold of humanity.
  Attend me!

Sallie Chesham

What About the Children?

Man in his madness makes mistakes and children have to pay,
Tomorrow's sorrow we produced by failing yesterday.
Man in his blindness blunders on and little children cry,
We have a right to please ourselves, that no one can deny.

But what about the children, the guiltless little children?
The children have to suffer because of our mistakes.
Let's think about the children, affrighted, blighted children,
And let's be better people for little children's sake.

by John Gowans
from Musical "Hosea"